Do you want to learn more about
***The Impulse Economy*? Sign up with Atria Books**
and get information directly from author
Gary Schwartz!

There are two ways to get to our sign-up page:

Text the keyword **IMPULSE** to **222377**
and we will send you a link to the sign-up page

or

Scan this code to go directly to the sign-up page

For a limited time you will have the opportunity to receive updated text and multimedia content from author Gary Schwartz related to *The Impulse Economy* directly to your phone, up to one message per month. Messages and data rates may apply to sending and receiving text messages, and/or to your use of the code. Consult your mobile carrier for applicable rates. **Text STOP to cancel and text HELP for help.** Terms and conditions at http://www.theimpulseeconomy.com/mobile.

**Do you want to learn more about
The Impulse Economy? Sign up with Atria Books
and get information directly from author
Gary Schwartz!**

There are two ways to get to our sign-up page:

Text the keyword **IMPULSE** to **222377**
and we will send you a link to the sign-up page

or

Scan this code to go directly to the sign-up page

For a limited time you will have the opportunity to receive updated text and multimedia content from author Gary Schwartz related to *The Impulse Economy* directly to your phone, up to one message per month. Messages and data rates may apply to sending and receiving text messages, and/or to your use of the code. Consult your mobile carrier for applicable rates. **Text STOP to cancel and text HELP for help.** Terms and conditions at http://www.theimpulseeconomy.com/mobile.

The Impulse Economy

Understanding Mobile Shoppers and What Makes Them Buy

Gary Schwartz

ATRIA BOOKS

NEW YORK LONDON TORONTO SYDNEY NEW DELHI

ATRIA BOOKS

A Division of Simon & Schuster, Inc.
1230 Avenue of the Americas
New York, NY 10020

First Atria Books hardcover edition October 2011

ATRIA B O O K S and colophon are trademarks of Simon & Schuster, Inc.

For information about special discounts for bulk purchases, please contact Simon & Schuster
Special Sales at 1-866-506-1949 or business@simonandschuster.com.

The Simon & Schuster Speakers Bureau can bring authors to your live event. For more information
or to book an event, contact the Simon & Schuster Speakers Bureau at 1-866-248-3049 or visit our
website at www.simonspeakers.com.

Designed by Timothy Shaner, nightanddaydesign.biz

Manufactured in the United States of America

23.45

10 9 8 7 6 5 4 3 2 1

Library of Congress Cataloging-in-Publication Data

Schwartz, Gary, 1964–
The impulse economy : understanding mobile shoppers and what makes them buy /
Gary Schwartz.
p. cm.
Includes bibliographical references and index.
1. Internet marketing. 2. Teleshopping. 3. Consumer behavior.
I. Title.
HF5415.1265.S385 2011
658.8'342—dc23 2011036957

ISBN 978-1-4516-7186-5
ISBN 978-1-4516-7188-9 (e-book)

Acknowledgments

I wrote much of this book over thousands of espressos, zig-zagging across cafés and airports throughout the United States. It is dedicated to my five children, whom I affectionately refer to as my mobile beta test team. They range in age from my seventeen-year-old, who can text with thumbs in the dark, to my one-year-old toddler, who thinks that all oblong objects are mobile phones and places every one she finds to her ear to say "'ello."

The big thanks goes out to the dozens of mobile, retail, commerce, and brand folk (far smarter than I) who took the time to steer me in the right direction.

Much of the writing and rewriting was reminiscent of director David Fincher's AT&T commercials that aired in 1993. He managed to predict e-books, tablets, E-ZPass, and in-car Global Positioning Systems. However, David still had phone booths in his version of the future. We proceed with caution.

Thanks to the bravado of industry folk like Facebook's Mark Zuckerberg and Google's Eric Schmidt, who proclaimed the death of e-mail and the end of plastic payment, respectively. And then not to forget John Henry Patterson, the father of the cash register and the inventor of the little bell that made every transaction go *ka-ching!*

No. 442. Price, $200

Contents

The
Impulse
Economy

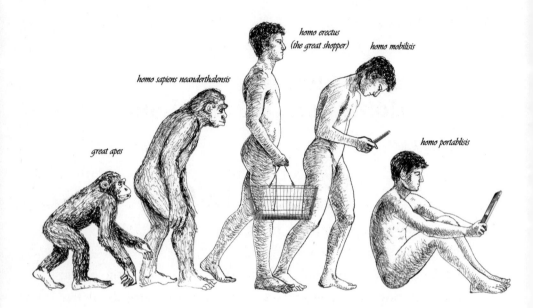

great apes

homo sapiens neanderthalensis

homo erectus
(the great shopper)

homo mobilisis

homo portablisis

Introducing the
Homunculus Handheld

In the 2010s, the mobile phone has become a digital hub where everything seems to converge: publishing, ticketing, media, wallets, banking, and shopping. In a world in which the mobile phone is intersecting and changing so many different verticals, it has become a sensory orthotic.

The mobile phone and mobile consumer increasingly appear to be merging. The two have become so intertwined that IBM Retail now regards "the consumer with their mobile phone" as one measurable instrument. As the phone becomes a seamless extension of our actions and our responses, the line separating the two becomes more blurred. While engineers try to eliminate the screen (tracking hand gestures and voice commands), designers optimize content navigation on the small screen.

The history of telephony is the history of minimizing barriers between user behavior and the phone. Freeing the consumer of the wire cord was one in a series of emancipations. Not many of us remember (or would even recognize) the first mobile phone prototype. It was trialed in the mid-1940s (questionably portable and definitely not practical). Used by the Swedish police and pow-

1

ered by the vehicle, this device could make six phone calls before it drained the squad-car battery.

Over the next five years, Ericsson managed to reduce the battery size to a dainty eighty pounds. It took thirty more years to develop a truly "mobile" phone. Motorola's catchily named DynaTAC 8000X, the world's first commercial handheld cellular, cost the company $100 million in research and development and weighed twenty-eight ounces. (Nicknamed the "brick," for obvious reasons.) Battery innovation and the move from analog to digital circuits paved the way for the first handheld devices that resembled the mobile phones we recognize today.

The future of the mobile phone seems aligned with Steve Jobs's vision of nothing but a perfect, borderless screen. Will mobile ultimately be the sum of embedded cranial telemetrics? Are we all becoming IBM instruments? Are we becoming one with our mobile phones? It is cyborg imagery like this that is the topic of dinner conversation across the United States.

And well it should be. Mobile data traffic is three times the size of the entire global Internet of 2000, when I started in wireless retail services. For an old Internet junky, this is mind-boggling. Our wireless data are fast becoming our consumer DNA. Billions of anonymous data points from our mobile phones are used daily to measure the flow of traffic on highways across the country. These red and green lines on traffic maps are the simplest examples of reading cumulative mobile consumer data.

Behavioral researchers can use mobile phone data to map the social interactions across multiple mobile devices. If you view these data as a superbrain with data synapses, you can predict the Dow Jones Industrial Average and political trends. By tracking changes in movement and communication patterns, the Massachu-

setts Institute of Technology (MIT) Human Dynamics Laboratory was able to detect a flu breakout before the students realized they were getting sick.

Much of these data are products of a smarter phone. The new smart data speak to anyone who chooses to listen: media planners, brands, retailers, and, of course, the consumer herself. These data have the ability to communicate complex and insightful information. The data hear, speak, see, store, and communicate everything that their owner prescribes. Collectively, the sum of all the phone data is the sum of the users' emotions, thoughts, and actions.

For years, the wireless carriers tried to retain control of the mobile subscriber by acting as a gatekeeper to external services and content. With the entry of the iPhone in 2007, the walls have come down. The consumer "decoupled" services from the network operators. The mobile value chain has opened up, and wireless carriers and handset and software vendors (as well as stakeholders in the banking and retail sectors) are rethinking their roles.

Players across the value chain are optimizing their mobile services to build a closer relationship with the consumer. eBay challenges its designers to enable a mobile bid in under fifteen seconds—the amount of time that a consumer may dwell at a red light or in an elevator. Best Buy challenges its Blueshirt consumer service team to be as mobile engaged as the shopper to compete for mind share in the store. Financial intuitions are battling to transform the phone into a mobile wallet to seamlessly TAP2PAY, while marketing departments attempt to use the same contactless technology to TAP2Coupon and TAP2WEB.

Brands, retailers, and services are not only competing for consumers but also for IBM's one measurable instrument that combines

the shopper, his phone, and his wallet. Mobile success stories in the coming year need to provide mobile-consumer insight, reach, engagement, and commerce. The marketer needs to master the impulse economy and provide solutions optimized for nanoseconds of nose-to-phone attention.

It is a high-stakes game where the winner is the one that ultimately controls the transaction (the mobile *ka-ching!*).

1 LITTLE STORE ON THE PRAIRIE

Your local store manager will tell you that there are two types of people: those who go to stores to buy specific items, and those who go to stores to shop. The history of retail, starting with the country store and moving to shopping malls, the Internet, and, more recently, mobile storefronts, is the history of following and serving these two types of shoppers.

Brand marketers and retailers compete for mind share. They woo their shoppers by price and brand affinity. These retailers also have segmented shoppers into groups that have profiles, patterns, and names: Alexa drops into the store for an item, but will browse opportunistically for other products. Suzy is self-directed, has a weekly shopping list and a mission. She motors down the aisle and out the store. Marge is store-directed and wants information on products first.

Marketing departments map the shopper's journey through their stores. They optimize the store layout and the shelf design. The US retail chain Target calls them "guests," Wal-Mart calls them "customers," and the clothing store Hot Topic calls them

"friends." Using Kroger's new mobile handheld, the supermarket chain's marketing department can see shoppers as icons moving pixel by pixel on a master store diagram.

Despite all the science, shopper marketing is a black art. Shoppers have what Ginger Kraus, vice president of brand activation at PlayStation, calls a "subsense," making decisions based on impulse and lifestyle. Each time that shoppers select a game console, walk into a fast-food restaurant, or reach out in the aisle to select a hair care product, there are a myriad of factors behind each decision.

What are the key factors that influence shoppers' behavior? How can marketers better understand shoppers? Finding the answers to these questions is what keeps brands and retailers up at night. To attempt this, we first need to understand the shopper's store and how it has changed over the past 120 years.

The Store Is A-Changin'

In the mid-nineteenth century, retail was a farmer's market. There were no stated prices and no customer satisfaction policies. The arrival of Main Street, with a concentration of shops and merchants, changed this model, and we saw prices and policy change almost hourly. By the time that Richard Sears appeared on the American retail scene in the late 1800s, the storefront had evolved to offer fixed prices and satisfaction guarantees with the promise of exchange or refund. Armed with these modern retail practices in place, Sears set out to build the modern store.

Indeed, Sears was instrumental in advancing the American shopping experience. Follow Sears, and you follow the evolution of the store. His success in retail was built on three principles: limitless shopping, self-serve shopping, and accessible shopping.

1. LIMITLESS SHOPPING

Richard Sears knew that American farmers typically bought supplies—often at inflated prices—from the local general store. Back in 1888, the first Sears catalogue provided a universal resource that clearly stated prices on a wide selection of goods. Consumers knew what Sears (then known as the R. W. Sears Watch Company) was selling and at what price, and could order goods conveniently without repeated buggy rides to the shop.

More important, Sears was no longer confined to a physical bricks-and-mortar presence. He could sell through the catalogue and was not limited to only what was in stock or on display in an aisle. For the American consumer, Sears quickly became *the* way to shop, and the catalogue became the "Consumer's Bible."

2. SELF-SERVE SHOPPING

Clarence Saunders brought the next wave of retail innovation when he moved the self-service efficiencies of the Sears catalogue back to the physical store. He patented the concept of the self-service shop and opened his first Piggly Wiggly grocery store in Memphis in 1916. Self-service made the store more cost-effective. Prices talked, and seven years later, there were 1,300 franchised locations across the United States.

In 1925, Sears, Roebuck and Co. followed the wave of retail chains opening across America by opening its first retail store. This was a far cry from the frontier general store concept that Sears had attacked successfully just a few decades earlier. This time the store was chock-full of modern efficiencies that would be further fine-tuned by Sam Walton, the founder of the Wal-Mart chain, later in the same century.

The stores were a draw, but the Sears catalogue continued to play an important role for shoppers. Specifically, Sears continued to use the catalogue as a way of dealing with the fact that aisles are limited in space and not always fully stocked. The catalogue provided shoppers with an always available list of goods that they could peruse, purchase, and have mailed to their doorsteps.

3. ACCESSIBLE SHOPPING

On November 27, 1995, Nathan Myhrvold, Microsoft's corporate visionary, wrote a memo to chief executive officer Bill Gates* warning that the Internet would allow companies to communicate directly with their end customers in a cheap and easy manner. This was a new retail model, he emphasized, and "it threatens the role of the middleman or pure merchant that traditionally sits between the large manufacturer of a good and the final customers." Myhrvold told Gates that he could no longer focus on selling software shrink-wrapped via Egghead Software; that this would become "quite ridiculous from an economic standpoint." Gates needed to consider a new model, a "'virtual Wal-Mart,' which presents goods directly to customers on the Internet, or via Internet catalogue kiosks in physical store locations."

Myhrvold's Internet was a natural extension of the shopping experience that Sears had revolutionized with the release of its first catalogues (although Sears may not have initially recognized it). In fact, the Internet has returned Sears to its roots. The Sears.com website mirrors the universal principals of shopping that Richard Sears advocated in 1895, when the catalogue had expanded to a hefty 350 pages of deals, more than any other approach. In many

*Ken Auletta, *New Yorker*, May 12, 1997.

ways, the Sears catalogue was the World Wide Web for the frontier consumer, and it continues to be that destination today.

This is because the Internet allows the Sears catalogue to be clickable. However, early prototypes of the website had few clicks. The first e-storefront was literally a cut-and-paste of the catalogue. As the digital store evolved, designers adapted bricks-and-mortar metaphors, such as the "shopping basket" and the "check out," for the web. The result was an ergonomically friendly click-through shopping experience.

Meanwhile, Wal-Mart efficiencies in the supply chain chipped away at the margins achieved by bricks-and-mortar stores across the United States, a phenomenon that quickly went global. Against this backdrop, Sears and other chains moved commerce into the cloud, chasing first movers such as Amazon.com and Yahoo!

The result was a hybrid model that brought together the concept of the limitless catalogue with the experience of in-store aisle roaming. Similar to shoppers who stroll leisurely through shopping malls, online shoppers had time to think and browse before they made their purchase. They cracked open the laptop late in the evening, when the kids were asleep and the dog was tucked under the chair. They had time to save their choices to a shopping basket. And they had time to do much more than just shop. They could compare prices, hunt for recommendations, e-mail their picks to friends and family members, and check out hours or days later.

Today limitless shopping, self-service shopping, and always accessible shopping are the hallmarks of the modern shopper's experience. The new Sears, like the old Sears, is not one destination; it is a menu of shopping options. Sears's "Shop your way—buy your way" approach is shoppercentric.

But does this make the physical store obsolete? "No," says Brett Bonner, who heads up store innovation at Kroger. "The history of the store is like a pendulum. The catalogue and, more recently, the Internet have offered alternative shopping channels to bricks and mortar. But we always return to the in-store shopping experience. We have incorporated this learning back into the store. It is the anchor.

"People forget that families used to get dressed up to go shopping," explains Bonner. "The store was the entertainment center of America. We thought that we would lose this to the catalogue and the Internet, but it didn't happen." In fact, he contends, the "pendulum is swinging again." This time it is paving the way for digital efficiencies to be reintroduced into the physical store experience.

Enter the Mobile Phone

As we review the many forms of retail that have emerged over the past 120 years, no one could have foreseen the rise of the m-shopper and the impact of mobile on the store. This new breed of consumer is using the mobile phone in the physical store to select products, research purchases, and act on deals and coupons at the point of decision.

This shopping revolution is in full force. While some in the retail industry recognize that the m-shopper has arrived, few have strategies in place aimed at capturing the m-commerce dollar. Misguided mobile web designers are working hard to adapt online shops and commerce functions to the constraints of the much smaller mobile screen. This approach overlooks the fact that mobile is more than just another screen. In fact, one of the reasons that

mobile commerce is perceived to be underperforming is not because m-consumption has not arrived or failed to ramp up. To the contrary, m-consumption has arrived and is thriving. Our mobile-commerce models are simply flawed or embryonic.

Cookie-cutter online assumptions to mobile don't guarantee revenue or conversion. While mobile presents a world of retail commerce opportunities, it can also be ineffective and underwhelm consumers. In some extreme examples, the experience can actually hinder shopping. Indeed, shoppers with their noses glued to the screen of their mobile phones shut out opportunities to engage effectively with the product. What's worse, mobile can even interrupt the shopper's purchase of this product.

However, if leveraged effectively, mobile enhances the shopper experience by allowing consumers to be open to impulse product selection in the aisle. We're already seeing the implementation of successful mobile services that overcome device shortcomings and free the shopper to be less nose-to-screen. In fact, new technology will allow shoppers to be completely untethered and 100 percent impulse driven.

Mobile is entering the in-store environment at a time when our idea of the store is changing dramatically. As we stroll, head bent, nose-to-screen, down busy streets and navigate the store aisle using peripheral vision, is the phone a homunculus guiding our shopping behavior, or is it a distraction, interrupting the design and the role of the store? This raises some interesting and critical questions about the future of retail. Some suggest that the historic *fight* for real estate in the store may ultimately trigger a *flight* of consumers from the store. Will the retailer's adversarial relationship with brands end up encouraging brands to pursue direct relationships with shoppers via their handheld devices? Or will

mobile help make the retail store more efficient and relevant to the modern shopper?

As we debate this, we face many challenges. Few industry insiders recognize the difference between a portable device and a mobile device, let alone how this affects the shopping experience. Even fewer recognize and accommodate the impulse-buying habits of the mobile shopper. And still fewer are generating anywhere near the potential revenue or reward that this new commerce platform has to offer.

It has the potential to become a perfect storm. Just not yet. That is what this book is about.

2 THE HISTORY OF THE MOBILE SHOPPER

I sat down with David Saltz in Las Vegas at the Mirage hotel and casino's High Limit Lounge, across from the mirrored entrance to Cirque du Soleil's *Love* production. Saltz, entertainment producer for the Mirage, has been the impresario of many mega-events, including Love, the mammoth 1985 Live Aid benefit concert, and, in 2007, Live Earth. Our discussion focused on mobile commerce. What works? How can Saltz leverage the mobile channel?

A few years back, the answer would have been simple: "premium mobile content." That's where the money and opportunity were. Remember ringtones? In the ringtone economy, mobile commerce was straightforward: text a short code and receive content. Billing happened transparently on the consumer's phone bill. Billions of dollars were made using direct billing—a few dollars at a time. Impulse buying was possible with no barrier, no hesitation, no fumbling for wallet and credit card details.

But Saltz wanted to know what formula would work in the *post*-ringtone economy. Now the answer is not so simple. If mobile

billing is not seamless (and charged to your phone bill), then it must happen via some other (tethered) payment mechanism such as credit cards. Effective and seamless mobile billing would require the payment channel (credit card) and the communication channel (phone) to be connected. What's more, they would have to be tied transparently, and without interrupting the shopping experience. They aren't.

Ironically, it is Vegas-savvy Saltz who should be solving the problem of mobile payments. Vegas is a master of the invisible hand. Casinos magically make the consumer experience contained and seamless. Once on the property floor, all payments are made fast and conveniently. There is no lining up with a shopping cart at the checkout. (No line-busting issues here.)

It struck me that with the end of the ringtone gold rush in North America and Europe, no mobile-commerce application or service had surfaced that came close to the boom period of the 2000s. What made the ringtone economy so successful? And who are the next mobile forty-niners?

Ringtone Revolution

Why did ringtone economics work? There were several simple economic principles in place. The magic was not the ringtone. It was driven by an explosion in consumer demand and the availability of seamless billing. Billing was key. In a world where music was becoming a commodity given away free of charge, ringtones (which consisted of a few seconds of severely degraded music track) sold for $2 apiece.

This was digital gold. A ten-second monophonic tune sold at a price point of $2 meant that the street value of the full track was

worth between $36 and $40. (And the average album would be worth upward of *$500*.) An even greater blessing for the beleaguered music executives: this $2 purchase had a half-life of one month before it was replaced by the next "hot" track. In addition, ringtones proved to be utterly price-inelastic. Consumers consistently were willing to pay for higher-priced ringtones over cheaper ringtones irrespective of the music selection.

As we drool over business models past, what can we learn? What are the commerce insights? Let's begin by looking at the carrier billing mechanism. Wireless carriers have a commercial advantage in that they hold the consumers' billing information. Consumers volunteer these data when they sign up for a phone subscription package or buy a prepaid card. The contractual relationship was necessary to enable the mobile operator to charge for its services. However, having this information also allowed the carrier to establish a simple banking mechanism for charging other services and content that consumers might purchase using their mobile phones.

The mobile industry has looked to the wireless carriers to innovate and launch new mobile services; however, in most cases, it has been the *consumers* (not the carriers) that have adopted and refined business models. The rise of SMS (short message service) texting is a prime example. The wireless carriers added a short alert protocol for pagers that allows messages to sneak through when bandwidth is available. Consumers adopted SMS early as a cheap alternative to paying expensive roaming costs. But the use spread beyond consumers on the move, a development that globally accelerated the use of texting to account for a larger chunk of the carriers' revenue. SMS became a dominant—and surprising—revenue windfall for the networks.

The runaway success of ringtones, like their cousin killer app SMS, could never have been anticipated. (Killer apps rarely are.) The first downloadable mobile ringtone was delivered to a consumer in Finland in 1998. Radiolinja (now Elisa) launched a service called Harmonium, providing tools for subscribers to create their own ringtones. The melodies were delivered over the air (OTA) via SMS to the consumer's mobile handset.

At the time, Ralph Simon, founder of Moviso (formerly Yourmobile, until Vivendi Universal purchased it in 2003 for $15 million and changed the name), was standing outside Helsinki's Hotel Kämp waiting for a taxi to the headquarters of Nokia, the Finnish mobile handset manufacturer. A local mobile innovator named Vesa-Matti Paananen pulled a mobile phone out of his jacket pocket. "I heard this mechanized sound," Simon recalled. "Like a tune that Lionel would play on his piano in a *Peanuts* cartoon. I was transfixed. I had just seen a person answer his phone's melody, *not* a ring."

The following day, Simon flew home to the United States and began meeting with music publishers to negotiate digital rights for the phone. However, this was one month after Napster, which pioneered peer-to-peer file sharing over the Internet, had rudely disrupted the music industry, and the reception was not warm. Stymied, Simon started using an offshore-rights agreement inked in Australia to deliver content to the US market through the cloud. Ralph was promptly sued for $90 million by EMI Music and demonized as a "pirate."

Over the next few months, with a free-to-consumer model and twenty million downloads, Simon and his team of Nicholas Rosenthal, Hilton Rosenthal, Anthony Stonefield, and tech wizard Shane Dewing were getting good press but running up further debt: $400,000 in SMS network fees alone. Still, Simon had proven

that there was a market, and his success attracted the attention of Sony Music. Jody Graham, the head of Sony/ATV Music Publishing, West Coast, allowed him to license its library, starting with the Beatles and Norah Jones. Within months, AT&T advanced him $2 million for a ringtone platform. An industry was born.

The mobile-commerce opportunity was magic, but the content was insipid. These monophonic data files had little more tonality than my five-year-old's Fisher-Price toy phone. But consumer desire for personalization seemed to override the quality of the music, and beeping and pinging ringtones became phenomenally successful.

In 2002 Nokia and other mobile phone companies adopted the MIDI (musical instrument digital interface) standard that enabled the creation of richer and more sonorous polyphonic music files—a welcome relief for anyone stuck with a popular person in a public space.

By 2003, polyphonic ringtones had earned their own sales chart in *Billboard* magazine, and $3 fees for these more sophisticated ringtones appeared on more monthly phone bills. That same year, Nokia introduced Nokia True Tones or Master Tones. This file format allowed mobile phones to play actual music, sound effects such as frog croaks, or a shout-out from your favorite pro basketball star. According to *Fortune* magazine, ringtones generated more than $2 billion in worldwide sales during 2005.

Why did ringtones rake in billions? This personalization currency was easy to consume. The carrier had, a priori, all the billing information it needed to enable the transaction. All that was required to make this high-margin business work was a demand for product. Prior to smart (web) phones, the wireless carrier controlled the consumer's mobile web navigation and category con-

tent. Consumers, not willing to thumb a long web address (URL) to go to a specific web destination, were more likely to follow the "carrier" control web shortcuts. This experience is called on-deck, and, of course, the carriers had a monopoly on this delivery channel. However, this portal advantage is fast disappearing as more ergonomically sound smartphones with bundled data packages put navigation back in the consumers' hands. This is called off-deck. The new on-deck equivalent is the APP* storefront, which handset manufacturers such as Apple (not the wireless carrier) now control.

Key to these mobile-commerce sales was the impulse nature of the purchase. The consumer simply texts a keyword to a short code (for example, TUNE1 to 101010) and instantly receives a link to download the ringtone. Within seconds, the phone rings to a custom tune. The pain of purchase is invisible and seamless. The ringtone is charged to the consumer's monthly mobile phone bill.

 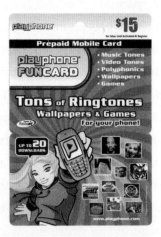

Purchase and content consumption all happened on your cell phone. The mobile channel was limited to high-margin digital

* I will capitalize the abbreviation *APP* to refer to "mobile" APPs, to differentiate them from traditional PC-based or server-side applications.

goods consumed on the phone (ringtones, graphics, horoscope) or to micropayment items (web access, virtual web credits). I recall walking into a wireless carrier in 2001 and proposing a joke-of-the-day subscription service. The biggest joke of all was that the consumer paid $1.25 per joke. Yet the service was a huge success. Lesson: suspend common sense with mobile services; the mobile consumer will opt in on impulse and pay for convenience. Today this micropayment economy, servicing video game and social network sites, is a healthy billion-dollar market.

However, the business model did not work for low-margin physical goods. Selling a concert T-shirt to a consumer on his mobile phone and billing the purchase to the monthly phone bill simply did not work. First, the business model was challenging, with the carrier taking up to 50 percent of the fee. Furthermore, with physical goods, there are unresolved tax and regulatory issues, not to mention the challenges of managing customer service when the carrier does not control the subscriber's experience end to end.

Until recently, wireless carriers such as AT&T and Verizon shied away from dealing in physical goods because delivery was far outside their control. Nor did they want to be a bank. Moving from digital and virtual goods to physical involved readjusting their business model. The leviathans' core business has always been focused on the consumer's voice and data plans. An irate consumer who paid for goods but did not receive them is a big problem.

- There is the $15 cost-per-customer service call.
- There is the dreaded fear of the customer's possibly switching to a competitive carrier.

Historically not worth the risk? As the wireless carriers belatedly discuss tweaking this revenue share model to accommodate virtual purchases online, Google and Apple seem to have co-opted the carrier digital business. Content has moved from ringtones to the new mobile-APP economy. Apple, Android, and the Nokia Ovi APP storefronts appear to be taking over the mobile pay walls. Pay walls block access and require payment to unlock the content.

Digital content plays such as Angry Birds and Farmville have used these new payment gateways to drive surprisingly lucrative businesses. Some, like Angry Birds, have a free "lite" version and a pay version. Others have in-APP billing for "free-mium" content (free access plus pay for premium-value add-ons like Farmville virtual chickens). The financial market looking for the next "ringtone revolution" is clamoring to invest in these start-ups. Zynga, the creator of Farmville, has raised a half billion dollars, giving it an eye-popping five-billion-dollar market cap.

The business model has opened up, but not enough to let in retailers of physical goods. From a 50 percent revenue share of premium SMS services, the Apple APP store takes 30 percent, while Android takes zero of the digital sale. This works for a digital-goods economy, where the download is the product. This works for virtual goods, where access to a website or virtual online currency is the product. However, how do retailers and brands drive commerce effectively on physical goods?

Impulse Economy

Malcolm Gladwell's best-selling book *Blink: The Power of Thinking Without Thinking* (2005) was such a commercial success because it explained (and, more significantly, justified) the importance of

our impulse decision making. Not only does Gladwell excuse our impulse behavior, he says that it is built into our genetic code. Intuition and instinct are *critical* to our survival. Thoughtful habits are not necessarily the best for humans. Forget the mountains of empirical facts and problem solving; Gladwell's contention is that "best decisions" are often made based on a few salient details within a second or two.

Back in 1996, pre-*Blink,* when Gladwell was a reporter for the *New Yorker* magazine, he wrote an article on "The Science of Shopping."* The subject of the article was retail guru Paco Underhill's research on shopper behavior. Underhill spent twenty years and countless hours observing unsuspecting shoppers though instore security footage. He found (among other factoids that we will discuss later) that shoppers walk on the same side of the aisle or concourse as they drive on the road. For Americans, of course, that means they bear right.

Based on Underhill's shopper insight, airports and malls across the United States position their fast-food restaurants on the left and gift shops on the right. Why? Because, according to Underhill, people may be willing to snake across a lane of pedestrian traffic for a meal, but they rarely cross the concourse to make an impulse buy of a candy bar or magazine. *Blink: The Power of Shopping Without Thinking?*

Clutter and *Ka-ching!*

Wal-Mart, JCPenney, Best Buy, and Dollar General have all remodeled their store floors to add clutter. They have been raising the

*www.gladwell.com/1996/1996_11_04_a_shopping.htm.

height of shelves, stacking stuff in the aisles, positioning items in empty corners. Yes, heaped bins are a cue for value and savings, but they also interrupt the shopping list and force impulse basket stuffing.

The science of shopping is the business of understanding and capitalizing on the shopper's intuitive actions: sometimes these actions are thoughtful and sometimes these actions are "blinks."

- The decision to cross the concourse chasm is thoughtful, I-can-do-it-later commerce; best left for the web storefront.
- The impulse purchase of the candy bar is mobile commerce: quick, easy, and within reach.

Mobile-shopping behavior is fast and impulsive. Slowing down the consumer in any way means possibly losing that consumer and any commerce opportunity. In other words, two clicks are one click too many for the mobile shopper. Mobile-shopper behavior needs to be based on pure muscle memory—or what Dawna Henderson, chief executive officer and president of the Henderson Bas Kohn advertising agency, calls Mobile Muscle Memory, or M^3.

The key to consumption is allowing mobile shoppers at the point of transaction to simply "blink," without the retailer over-burdening them with commerce questions. Check-out procedures that require too much time filling out forms, too much time searching a purse, will lead to abandoned shopping carts. Although we know this about the shopper, how do we dispense with collecting the all-important billing information? The magic of ringtone consumption was the ability of the wireless carrier to remove any visible pain of payment. The charge is deferred to the phone bill's arrival at the end of the month.

It is unquestionably one of the reasons for the success of the multibillion-dollar ringtone market, as well as an inhibitor to its successor, the mobile storefront market. It is all about reducing steps, seamless billing, and deferred billing.

ABI Research, a technology market intelligence company, notes that mobile shopping in the United States soared from $396 million in 2008, to $1.2 billion in 2009, to $2.4 billion in 2010. However, only 5 percent of web purchases are made via the handheld device. This is a fraction of the market potential. US consumers who are using their mobile phones to compare prices in store do not seem to be converting this to mobile purchases.

Most pundits write that increased smartphone use, as well as the growth of mobile-commerce websites, will continue to spur the US market's growth. While e-commerce folk saw their Black Friday mobile sales spike from 0.01 percent in 2009 to 5.6 percent in 2010, trending is not as aggressive as it could and should be.

ABI Research indicates that by 2015, shoppers around the world are expected to spend about $119 billion on goods and services bought via mobile phones; that's 8 percent of the total projected e-commerce market. However, these numbers are no indication that mobile commerce will parallel this trend in the United States and Europe without significant changes in the ease of commerce at the point of decision.

Although Japan's mobile commerce is up tenfold (20 percent of Tokyo's digital shopping is done via the phone), it is questionable whether a parallel can be drawn in North America. For one thing, in Japan, mobile is one of the only means to access the Internet. In the United States and Europe, we cannot force m-commerce adoption via necessity. We need to drive adoption via convenience and ease.

We need to understand that mobile commerce is not only about payment but the ability to optimize the path to this payment. Farhan Ahmad, director of emerging payments at Discover Financial Services, the issuer of the Discover Card, the third largest credit card brand in the United States, explains, "Mobile payment is a small subset of mobile commerce. Mobile commerce is primarily about shopper engagement and marketing."

So let's look at what drives mobile-like impulse purchases in the bricks-and-mortar checkout. Two factors seem to come into play:

1. PROXIMITY TO WALLET

Step into a Kroger or Safeway, and you'll notice that all store managers recognize that some goods have a greater potential to be bought on impulse than others do. These items are usually positioned strategically at checkout.

The prepaid mall—the rack of plastic gift cards at the entrance of many retail stores in North America—boasts the highest margin per square inch of any real estate in the store. Like confectionery and grab-and-run magazines, they help top off the shopper's grocery basket at checkout and top off the retailer's margin.

No one seems able to explain definitively why the buyer is myopic at the point of sale or why certain items are more readily consumed, but I would guess that the shopper's having his wallet open and being ready to pay is one factor. Purchases of candy and magazines at the cash register admittedly have more to do with the products' proximity than their merits.

2. MINIMIZING CHOICE

In Sheena Iyengar's 2010 book *The Art of Choosing*, she discusses the "too much choice problem." Having a wide selection of products—let's say, brands of jams—may appear optimal for the shopper; however, even the most jam-deprived person will be stupefied in front of an overly large selection. According to Iyengar, a business professor at Columbia University, more shoppers will buy jam if they are presented with a limited selection. Too many choices can be debilitating, ultimately convincing consumers to choose not to choose.

With a larger selection of products found on the web in the endless aisle, we rely on social recommendation tools to navigate the options, including e-mail, instant messaging, social networks, and parking your shopping cart to chat with your partner.

We need a mobile-optimized path to purchasing. Mobile does not offer these multitasking options as readily. We are parked for good unless the process is distilled.

John Thompson, senior vice president and general manager of Best Buy, calls this the "tyranny of more." He stresses that the store needs to eliminate complexity, advising, "Give abundance of choices, but also offer the tools to help the shoppers find the right thing for them."

The twenty-first-century American consumer has been bombarded by the impulse demons of shopping malls, online storefronts, and now the very phone in his pocket. The phone, if correctly used, is the ultimate black art. If any commerce platform will move the American consumer further from his prairie general store roots, it is the mobile phone.

How do we get there?

The Day Haiti Changed
M-Commerce Forever

So what is the m-commerce dream? To enable seamless purchase at the point of decision? Retailers and manufacturers are all poised to capitalize on this channel. It will come, and the response to the Haiti earthquake in 2010 was a good barometer.

Mobile donation services started back in the late summer of 2005. When I first met Jim Manis, CEO of the Mobile Giving Foundation, he was working at m-Qube, trying to set up a mobile donation channel during the Hurricane Katrina crisis that devastated New Orleans. We were trying to run a benefit concert at New York's Madison Square Garden. Verizon Wireless was the first company out of the gate to allow consumers to donate via mobile to the American Red Cross by text messaging the short code 2HELP (24357). But the process, though admirable, was ad hoc. There were no taxable receipts or standard way of donating on all wireless carriers in the United States.

When a Colorado entrepreneur named James Eberhard put mobile donations on the drawing board three years later, he hooked up with Manis and created the mGive Foundation and the Mobile Giving Foundation. The two foundations offered a simple one-stop platform for charities to launch donation services across every national major carrier.

Red Cross mobile donation results are testament to the success of this impulse-payment channel. When the earthquake devastation hit Haiti, consumers could reach for the phone and donate $10 just by texting HAITI to 90999 to donate $10. The donation was seamlessly billed to their phone and appeared on the January 2010 bill. Taxable receipts could be printed online by simply entering the donor's mobile phone number.

Within one day after the earthquake hit Haiti on January 12, $1 million was raised through microdonations via SMS, and within three days, the number was nearly $20 million—all in $10 contributions. We also saw donation requests on prime-time television (with NFL players touting their phones) that solely mentioned the SMS channel: *no* call-in number, *no* website address. Once the word was in the market, the simple mobile call to action allowed for peer-to-peer organic, flash viral growth. (Illustratively, when Japan was rocked by the largest earthquake in its history, followed by a tsunami, in March 2011, people *organically* began twittering the same SMS donation call to action, and funds started pouring in once again.)

Does $40 million in microdonations to Haiti relief via the cell phone finally demonstrate the power of a native mobile-commerce channel? What we must learn from the Haiti relief effort is how to influence consumer behavior. We need to find a viable billing solution that will drive the same impulse behavior as SMS donation services. This donation channel has taught us that in our impulse mobile economy, products and services cannot and should not be buried behind storefronts and phone lines. What Haiti also taught us is that communication and commerce should start on simple, instant channels.

It was no surprise when Facebook founder Mark Zuckerberg said, "E-mail is dead." Like a voice call (and its historic antecedent, the letter), e-mails still require undue time and formality. In our impulse economy, anything that distracts, masks, or slows down the message should be eliminated.

For example, the popularity of the *R* for "message read" in BlackBerry Messenger (BBM), the popular instant-messaging service, indicates the universal demand for instant response. Like-

wise, Apple's iMessenger is new age mail (hit the thought button and immediately fire off the message), while Twitter is new age instant microblogging.

How does the retailer become part of this conversation?

Bells and Whistles Versus Reach and Frequency

The Haiti crisis also underscored that mobile successes often demand a large, captive consumer community, an install base, that can offer reach and in-market frequency. "For mobile to matter," says Paul Gunning, CEO of the ad agency Tribal DDB Worldwide, "mobile needs scale. We need to be running campaigns that can reach fifty million people for the industry to become a major media channel."

Reach is fundamental to any mobile discussion. To illustrate this, let's compare two elections on two continents. In April 2007 a nonprofit organization called the Network of Mobile Election Monitors (NMEM) set out to empower Nigerian citizens to monitor the results of their country's presidential election by sending on-the-ground reports via SMS messages. It seemed a good idea in a country of nearly one million square kilometers with thirty million phones and a few foreign observers running around in UN-branded jeeps and T-shirts emblazoned with the word *Observer*.

Fast-forward to the 2008 US presidential election. With all the mobile marketing bravado, a citizen-journalist program called Video the Vote (www.videothevote.org) was put in place. The goal was to record any disruption or fraudulent activity in the voting process. It had the same goals as the Nigerian monitoring campaign: lots of polling booths, lots of people, lots of phones. Upload your mobile footage and keep America free.

Although the average US citizen had a camera-equipped phone at the time, what actually worked during the election could have been run off basic Nokia 100 phones twenty years earlier. This begs the question: Do all the bells and whistles of the new age phone really change the consumer's core behavior? SMS donations allow for ubiquitous reach and just-in-time decision making.

In order for the 2012 US presidential race to succeed in reaching the voting mobile American, it will need to leverage simple accessible channels. According to the digital marketing research company InsightExpress, as of September 2010, non-smartphone owners used their phones primarily as a messaging device. When you look at smartphone usage, messaging usage just continues to grow, shooting to 78 percent. It is clear that messaging and the mobile web are the channels of choice.

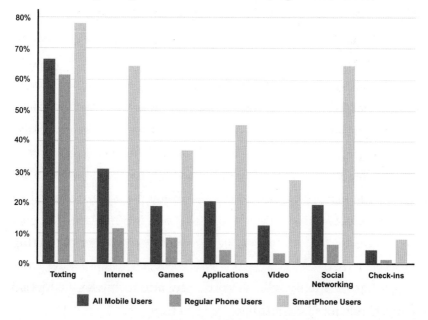

Weekly Usage of Mobile Features (September 2010)

Source: InsightExpress's Mobile Consumer Research, September 2010

Now, while mobile statistics are used to justify many questionable trends in the economy (I think the adage is "If you torture data enough, it will confess to anything"), one development that remains impervious to change is the adoption and growth of messaging.

According to the venerable Nielsen Company, the average US consumer texts six hundred times per month, compared to using fewer than than two hundred voice minutes. That adds up to more than five billion text messages each day.

Text interaction with brands continues to increase: in 2007 roughly one in six people signed up for some sort of text alert. In 2009 that number was one in five, with significant increases in sign-ups from men and women ages eighteen to forty-four.

Signed Up for Some Text Alert

	Gen Y	Gen X	Young Boomers	Older Boomers
Signed up for some text alert	**32%**	**27%**	**19%**	**15%**
Airlines	5%	7%	7%	5%
Music groups	10%	6%	3%	0%
Restaurants or bars	5%	6%	4%	2%
Food/drink products	6%	5%	2%	1%
Radio stations	10%	6%	3%	0%
Weather	16%	13%	11%	7%
Magazines	5%	5%	1%	0%
Sports	7%	10%	6%	2%
Traffic	5%	7%	2%	3%
Other	5%	5%	4%	4%

Source: InsightExpress's Mobile Consumer Research, July 2010

We are a simple folk. Accordingly, our technology-adoption patterns seem to be constant:

1. Two clicks are one click too many.
2. I use only services that help me effectively
 - kill time.
 - save time.
 - save money.
3. Instant communication makes me feel good.

Put most of our technology innovations through this filter, and you will see if they will succeed or fail.

With regard to the Haiti relief effort, you can check 1, 2b, and 3.

Ringtone economics are long forgotten, and media companies are in heated discussion over mobile APPs and other leading-edge ways to engage the consumer. The reality is that what we debate and what actually works are often two different things. We now agree (if you drink my Kool-Aid) that the mobile business has historically been driven by unassuming but universally adopted communications solutions.

There are peer-to-peer messaging channels such as iMessage, BlackBerry Messenger, Google's Huddle, and Facebook Messenger. There are incredibly successful group messaging services like Text-Plus and BlackBerry Messaging Groups, which allow one message to instantly reach a whole group. There are open channels for brands such as Twitter, SMS, multimedia messaging service (MMS), and Facebook and APP alerts. These are all essential ingredients of communicating and being communicated with by the shopper.

The messaging channels that allow for the most reach and the closest two-way relationships with the phone number are SMS and MMS. Text messaging may not be as inspiring as the razzle-dazzle of other channels, but it has become a dominant form of communication. As Doug Busk, the head of global mobile strategy for Coca-

Cola, points out, more than 6 trillion messages are sent around the planet every year (trending to double every 18 months).

Mickey Khan, editor in chief of *Mobile Commerce Daily,* sums it up by saying, "Tapping the existing customer base to sign up for opted-in SMS alerts is the logical first step. The next is to build this relationship with offers that really matter to the opted-in consumer. Retailers simply need to look to Wal-Mart. The Wal-Mart SMS short code costs only $500 per month to lease in the United States— chicken feed for a retailer whose annual sales last year were $404 billion. SMS can stoke desire, even if it's not eye-candy material."

> FREE MSG: Wal-Mart Rollbacks. 17–21 oz Frosted Flakes, Froot Loops, Corn Pops & Apple Jacks now $2.94, was $3.28. Reply HELP for Help; STOP to Cancel.

> FREE MSG: Wal-Mart Rollbacks. 24 pk 12-oz cans of Coke, Pepsi & Dr Pepper for just $5. That's $.25 per can. Price may vary in OK, WI, HI, AK, NY, PR & CT.

"Retailers sometimes miss the wood for the trees, fussing over elaborate mobile measures, when the easiest and the first step should be creating an SMS program backed by a memorable short code and keywords," says Khan.

I tested his assumption with a major US retailer. I sent a retail offer to an e-mail group and an SMS group, segmented equally according to size and demographic—a simple A/B test. With this retailer, we used its affinity program to measured closed-loop converse to the store. Eight out of one hundred folk who received the offer via e-mail went and bought the product; 8 percent conversion is remarkably good for e-mail. The SMS group, however, drove 22 percent conversion: nearly three times the success of the e-mail response.

3 WHEN TO POP THE COMMERCE QUESTION?

I was in China twenty years ago, filming a documentary on the last Chinese Jews of the old trading city K'ai-feng, located just south of Beijing. Between shoots, while I was exploring the city by walking the outdoor markets, I came across a new shopping complex that had one odd feature.

It was a normal, bustling department store. However, as I approached the center of the building, there appeared to be a disturbance. Strangely, security officers manned the top and the bottom of the moving metal stairs and a line of would-be shoppers on each end. Shoppers were jumping, tripping, falling down the escalator.

After watching people moonwalk and bound on and off the moving stairs into the arms of the security team, I turned to a formally dressed officer. In fumbling Chinese, I asked him what institution these shoppers been shipped in from. It turned out that this was the first escalator installed in K'ai-feng, and no one had ever used moving metal stairs before. Hard to believe for someone who grew up on shopping mall escalators, but illustrative of how

much of a barrier a new convenience can be to the unsuspecting shopper. The simplest things for the initiated-service community will not be easily adopted by the shopper.

In all technology areas, solutions that work provide some small, incremental value to business as usual. Revolutions take place, but they sometimes happen in fumbling, small steps.

We have reached an inflection point with m-commerce, but we seem uncertain on how to use the phone as an m-wallet. The sheer number of shoppers that are primed for the mobile wallet is astounding. According to the GSMA, by 2013, 1.7 billion mobile phone users will not have a traditional fixed bank account. Mobile subscriber penetration worldwide will continue to increase, with over 5.4 billion handsets expected to be in circulation by the end of 2015.

In Africa, remarkably successful mPESA (*m* for mobile; *pesa* is Swahili for money) services have allowed Africans to shop and pay over their mobile phones. Their counterparts in Europe and North America seem less comfortable making physical transactions on the mobile phone. Coca-Cola and other commerce-hungry brands are looking to mPESA in Africa to aggressively drive beverage purchases through mobile peer-to-peer micropayments. However, outside of a few mobile-enabled Coke vending machines in the developing world, Coke's m-commerce goals in North America are more modest.

We have read articles of South Korean commuters using their phones to purchase neon-backlit cabbages and cucumbers that are neatly selected-packed-delivered in the cloud. Should we expect this in our neighborhood in the near future? Will new, contactless phone wallets allow Tesco Homeplus brand to export its South Korean virtual grocery service to the United States?

I would have to say not beyond a novelty trial. Shoppers and their shopkeepers are slow to change. We like to prod and poke our cabbages and cucumbers.

In North America, when shoppers were asked how they would use their device when looking to purchase physical goods, they prioritized price comparison, search, and research activities far above the ability to make an actual purchase.

Mobile Shopping Behavior

Digital Purchase	Virtual Purchase	Physical Purchase
1. Price Comparison	1. Research	1. Price Comparison
2. Purchase	2. Price Comparison	2. Local Store
3. Research	3. Purchase	3. Search
	4. Local Store	4. Research
	5. Search	5. Purchase

Source: Informa WCIS Q4 2010, inMobi Mobile Shopping Research, March 2010

Why? Well, one simple reason is that there are different environmental factors globally and mobile models cannot be wholesalely imported. mPESA is helping displace the standard practice of carrying and paying with cash. There are few credit and debit cards on the African continent. In the United States, however, credit and debit cards displaced checks, not cash. Cash as a payment choice has held fairly constant over the past fifty years.

Irrespective of the payment types and flavor of commerce we adopt in North America, some form of mobile wallet will become part of our shopping experience. Success hinges on when and how the industry pops the commerce question to the would-be shopper. Mobile wallets are unnaturally personal places, tied to our social

personality, our social identity, and, more important, our communication channel. However challenging, successfully establishing an m-wallet relationship is worth any effort. Pairing mobile commerce with a customer relationship (CRM) is the coveted goal of any retailer and brand.

There are three in-market mobile wallets:

- carrier wallet (payment via the wireless carrier bill),
- proximity wallet (contactless mobile payment),
- quick-checkout wallet (traditional payment optimized for the mobile phone).

Each is tied to specific goods, limited to certain business models, adopted by different demographics, and has varied maturity and reach in the market.

Carrier Wallet: The Arranged Date

Some mobile-commerce relationships are like arranged dates. The consumer and the merchant know what is expected from the outset. Take the relationship with a wireless carrier: The billing relationship is bundled with the AT&T or Verizon contract. The consumer provides a billing mechanism for the carrier to bill on a monthly basis. This allows the carrier to charge for other in-channel content such as ringtones, data, chat, and other services.

When a consumer signs up for a phone on a wireless network, he or she is essentially opening a bank account to debit against. Prepaid accounts have turned many wireless carriers into micropayment megabanks. Vodafone, a major wireless carrier in Europe,

has 350 million subscribers, 80 percent with prepaid accounts, and with an average of 25 euros on the card equal to billions on deposit at any given time. This means the wireless carrier has a whopping $5 billion to $7 billion in reserve for its consumers to debit.

It is implicit in this relationship that the phone bill is open to a smorgasbord of commerce options. The consumer and the bank (carrier) are on a date with their eyes wide open. Stuff will happen, and bills will grow with miscellaneous purchases.

But there are limitations to this SMS-based-billing channel (premium SMS). Commerce is relegated largely to microtransactions. Beyond ringtones and graphics to personalize the consumer's phone, payment companies such as Boku, Paymate, and Zong use SMS commerce to allow consumers to pay for small virtual items. Although short message service was not initially built or structured to manage payments for virtual goods and website access, they have found a billing niche that is simpler for many than using their traditional wallet. Consumers enter their mobile phone number on a website and get a validation PIN. Input this PIN on the webpage, and—*Bam!*—commerce on their phone bill. They can now log in with their avatar in SmallWorlds, check in at a virtual Zong ATM, and withdraw virtual coins to buy a virtual drink for a virtual friend. All thanks to simple payments made to their phone bill.

In the United States, major carriers have expanded the size of the micropayment wallet. Sprint, AT&T, and Verizon have launched services that enable a $25 monthly debit account on customers' phone bills. Consumers can draw down from this amount for microtransactions.

Brave New World

In a new world where wireless networks feel a trifle unloved, certain carriers in partnership with the GSMA are regrouping to develop a set of APIs (application program interfaces) that go beyond SMS billing. These wireless carriers, anxious to avoid being treated as "dumb pipe" networks (networks that have no value-added service offering), are trying develop a cross-carrier one-stop shop to expose useful network information and capabilities to web application developers. The initial focus is on location and messaging services. More services may follow.

At the 2010 Mobile World Congress, the Wholesale Applications Community (WAC) was announced, with the purpose of promoting the use of web technologies to enable developers to write a single application that can run across multiple mobile-device platforms. This will allow developers to deploy a single application across multiple devices through the use of standard technologies and across multiple operators without the need to negotiate with each of them.

To make these APIs more business ready, mobile organizations such as the Mobile Entertainment Forum (MEF) are working to create business models showing how application program interfaces (APIs) are used in practice through its Smart Enablers Initiative, in which content owners, aggregators, and network operators work together to look at practical issues and business models and determine the most important APIs that content owners need from networks. MEF's work is nontechnical and will feed into the GSMA OneAPI project. O2 and Vodafone are working with the MEF to build business models for services such as location, user presence, age verification, sender-pays data, user demographic profiles, and mobile wallets.

Digital, Virtual, but Little Physical

Proliferation of screens and the ubiquity of connected platforms will make the term *mobile payment* somewhat blurred, as almost all devices will be interactive, wireless, and connected to the user's digital life—everything will be "mobile enabled." There are cer-

tain payments, goods, and phone interfaces that are optimized for wireless carrier billing, while others are better supported by tethered payment methods with various security verification channels.

The following chart shows examples of services that are *within* the wireless carriers. There are examples of goods that are bought, the type of goods, how the purchase is secured, and the funding source.

Goods	Type	Transport	Funding
• Horoscope	• Digital	• SMS / MMS	• Carrier Bill
• Web Access	• Virtual	• WAP Billing	• Carrier Bill
• Game APP	• Digital	• APP Store	• Credit Card
• Coupon	• Virtual	• QR Code	• Stored Value

The bulk of mobile transactions are still relegated to digital and virtual services accessed on the phone or online. Carriers have optimized billing beyond premium SMS, allowing the vendor to make seamless payments without switching billing modalities to SMS; however, all these solutions are still tailored to high-margin goods and services, which limit their applicability to traditional retailers in the physical world. Physical purchases of, say, shoes are outside the carrier billing world.

Joe Lynam is one of many in the industry trying to change this. Joe started PaymentOne, a US payment solution provider, in 1998 with a $35 million commitment from AOL to place its $20 monthly subscription fee on users' home phone bills. Joe exchanged billing war stories with me over a glass of wine in downtown Palo Alto, California. "What's old is new again," he observed. "What we managed to do ten years ago with the wire-line carriers is still

the most obvious billing model now—it is so simple to bill to an existing account."

Many companies are trying to expand the carrier wallet with better business terms that would allow for a wider selection of products and services that could be billed directly to the phone bill. Then there are industry disrupters such as Payfone, which has taken things a step further by actually becoming a virtual carrier (like AT&T or Verizon). Payfone uses the carrier-to-carrier roaming agreements globally to facilitate payment for goods to multiple carrier phone bills.

Payforit is a similar billing initiative out of the United Kingdom. The user simply hits a link and agrees to make a purchase, after which he or she can download content that is charged directly to the phone bill. Payforit leverages billing directly through the mobile browser. Using billing via the phone, shoppers can perform micro-transactions with one click, without registering for a service or dealing with a username or a password. The initiative was first announced in March 2006 and is supported by all UK mobile operators.

All these solutions are ideal for in-browser activity, as the user doesn't need to switch modalities to premium SMS to charge to the phone bill. PaymentOne, Payforit, Payfone, and many other payment vendors working with the wireless carriers require one final step to succeed: a business model that would allow for physical goods to be sold. In the interim, bill-to-carrier payment services will help consumers utilize mobile payment for virtual and/or physical services such as movie tickets, parking meters, train and bus fares, and other frequent convenience services that can be scanned off the phone. With the recent purchase of Zong by PayPal, it is clear the dust has not settled on this turf war.

Proximity Wallet: The Brazen Pickup

If we try to go outside of the existing bill-to-phone relationship, then we need to ask consumers to tether their phones to an existing payment method—the kind that you would find in your wallet. Visa, MasterCard, and other commerce giants see their futures in physically embedding or attaching secure payment into the phone. For Visa's payWave and MasterCard's PayPass to succeed on the mobile network, they need to be simple and seamless enough to spur consumer adoption.

We have fought and won this battle before. The first credit card was the Diners' Club, issued to two hundred folk in New York City in 1950. It was a nonwipable, nontapable piece of cardstock paper. One year later, there were twenty thousand cards in circulation.

The efficiencies and security of plastic payment with ironed-on magnetic identification strips did not come into existence until the mid-1960s, with the rise of the modern credit card. Visa and MasterCard (originally called Master Charge) are joint ventures—miraculous examples of business cooperation across multiple sectors. These joint ventures were owned by competitive banks that

remain competitors in all aspects of the business but worked together to set standards and allow consumers to use the same cards locally and globally at all major retailers.

David Evans and Richard Schmalensee detail this unlikely, somewhat collusionary tale in their history of the plastic wallet, *Paying with Plastic: The Digital Revolution in Buying and Borrowing.* Evans and Schmalensee use the term "two-sided business" to describe two groups of people who have complementary needs but no way to meet those needs without a common ground. The history of plastic and the business machinations needed in the sixties to launch services globally makes for a model that the mobile payment industry should be studying.

Creating the service was a huge feat; consumer acceptance was an even greater achievement. In order for the shopper to move from paper to plastic and now from plastic to phone, all forces need to align for the common business weal.

Show Me Some *Ka-ching!*

The battle to move plastic to more fluid mobile currency has been raging for some time. Financial services providers are working hard to make plastic (credit, debit, stored-value, loyalty) virtual and interactive. With all this industry chatter, why are we not seeing more in-market examples of these services?

Trials are not new. The first mobile contactless payment pilot program started in 2003, and many other pilots have come along since. The industry is working hard to develop protocols to secure mobile payments at a comparable level to plastic payments. Eight years later, we are seeing some of the results coming to market internationally.

One of the main challenges that the banking community has faced is authenticating a payment or stored value on your mobile device. They need to find a simple and secure way to connect this device to a party who can verify and settle this payment or voucher. There are many strategies to bridge this physical gap remotely. Starbucks scans a trackable 2-D code on the screen of the phone. PayPal's Bump uses an accelerometer. If that doesn't work, Fig Card, a PayPal company, provides shopkeepers with a USB that communicates with a downloadable mobile APP over a store's Wi-Fi network. Shopkick uses hardware that emits special frequency sound waves. The payment landscape is so confused that Visa has bet on conflicting payment strategies, concurrently investing in mobile hardware companies (for example, Square) and at the same time cloud-based companies (for example, Playspan). With all this costly and confusing bubblegum and shoelace, many consumers and retailers may dispense with physical m-checkout and just look to the cloud for a mobile web checkout.

Over the past few years, near field communication (NFC) is emerging as the solution du jour for connecting the phone to a transaction at the point of purchase. NFC is a machine-to-machine short-range wireless-connectivity payments system. NFC is a secure protocol that sits on top of the *same* tagging technology that is used to track household pets and makes an unpaid-for item beep when exiting a shop. We call this radio-frequency identification, or RFID, and it can be used to enable a two-way communication channel for multiple services.

The RFID tags are powerful things. They can be passive identification coils embedded in food packaging, circulars, street posters, medicines, clothing tags, and much more. The reader or scanning antenna provides the tag with the energy to communicate. Passive

RFID tags do not need to contain batteries and can remain usable for very long periods—up to decades. Interestingly, the first RFID case studies involved tracking nuclear materials.

There are so many wireless protocols, from Wi-Fi to Bluetooth, that it is confusing even for an industry person. How is NFC different from other major standards? You need to consider the original purpose of the protocol and look at frequency range and limitations.

- **INFRARED** allows for exchange of data over infrared light (range: less than one meter with line of sight).
- **BLUETOOTH** was designed to replace cables between communication devices (range: ten meters).
- **WI-FI** was designed and optimized for local area networks (LAN); it provides an extension or replacement of wired networks for dozens of computing devices (range: more than one hundred meters).
- **RFID** (radio-frequency identification) is an automatic identification method that stores and retrieves data via RFID tags. An RFID tag is a small object that contains silicon chips that can be attached to or incorporated into a product.
 - **Passive RFID** does not have its own power source (range: ten centimeters to one hundred meters if it passes through a strong enough field isolated from sources of interference).
 - **Active RFID** has its own power but otherwise follows RFID protocol; it may have sufficient range to be tracked by satellite. NFC is similarly affected by the power of the reader-transceiver. It is amazing what a good directional, tunable antenna with high-power amplifiers can do.

- **CONTACTLESS SMART CARDS** embed a chip that communicates with a card reader via the above RFID technology (range: ten centimeters).

Devices containing RFID are triggered by proximity. (Proximity is defined by the strength of the scanning device; the stronger the scanner, the stronger the RFID signal is amplified. It reflects the evolution of early radar technology.)

Think of wanding your phone to enter a subway or a movie to pay for services. This is called contactless payments, or proximity payment: convenient "tap and go." NFC passes very short messages (like a URL or a token) so that two devices can uniquely identify each other. Once it has done this, the device can proceed to fulfill payment, provision coupons, download content, and so on. If you have near field communication attached in some manner to your phone, it can read and write to a cash register in the store, it can exchange data from one device to another, and it can store data (tickets, coupons) that can be read by an NFC-enabled device. BMW is even putting them into its car keys to allow for tap-pay-and-drive functionality.

NFC can be used in three ways:

- **PAYMENT**: If the *phone is the tag*, it can be used to make the phone a form of secure identification and payment. This tag allows the phone to be a key to access your office as well as to be used as your mobile-wallet credentials.
- **MARKETING**: If the *phone is the reader*, NFC can read external tags to allow for tap-to-web, tap-to-coupon proximity. In this case, the tag is on the media or product.

- **PEER-TO-PEER**: The phone is the reader and writer allowing for TAP file transfer from one handset to another. Thus the phone can be used to transfer shopping lists, business cards, and so forth.

Creating NFC phones elegantly bundled with an activated bank account is not a simple proposition. Proximity marketing may be the first to see traction.

While the industry is seemingly embracing NFC as the retail payment standard by conducting high-visibility trials in the market, piles of logistics and business issues still must be resolved. Banking fragmentation and retail lethargy make it difficult to see past the PR, and having so many stakeholders in the value chain does not help. As plastic cards will not disappear any time soon, any mobile payment solutions will need to work in parallel with existing payment systems and major processors and be enabled at the majority of retail checkouts.

Everything Everywhere:
The Battle for the M-Wallet

PayPal, the online payment incumbent, is taking legal action against Google Wallet, the new Android-phone payment solution. It is the opening salvo of many battles that will rage for a number of years, with various players posturing and staking ownership of the wallet. The technology is not the challenge. There are only a few ways to attach the wallet to the phone, but each method favors a different player in the payment value chain. The winner takes all.

STICKERS: A simple way of making a phone into a wallet is a sticker with an embedded chip that can be attached to the back of your phone. While this is not an elegant solution, it cuts through the mess of players in the value chain that need to all "play nice" in order to have the payment prebundled with the phone. While the consumer can manage the account via the phone browser and receive payment alerts to the phone via SMS, it is a disjointed experience.

Over the past few years, we have seen stickers bundled as a "daughter card" of an existing payment card—that is, a card addressing the same user account as a primary card. In 2008, Best Buy teamed up with MasterCard to run the most comprehensive early trial of 50,000 payment stickers with their premium shopper community with (what they consider) great success. The Bling Nation's "Bling Tag" sticker trial in Palo Alto similarly couples the phone to the consumer's PayPal account. Although it has worked smoothly with participating Palo Alto retailers it may not be extensible to mainstream US trials. In all tag trials, the only connection with the phone and the payment sticker is the adhesive. This is a mobile hitchhiker, no more native to the phone than a

plastic contactless card cruising around in your pocket. Many in the financial services industry see this as a test phase to gauge consumer and retail adoption.

SIDE LOADING: A more integrated method for securing a banking account to the phone is to embed a chip into its removable memory card. MicroSD cards can be personalized with the bank name, look like a mini–credit card, and can be processed through the existing banking infrastructure. Bank NFC stickers have a specifically designed antenna combined with a ferrite backing layer to cut distortion to and from the phone's components and its radio signal. There are "active stickers" on the market that can establish a connection between the sticker and the phone user interface (UI) through Bluetooth. Active stickers enable a connection to the phone operating system and user interface, which makes the sticker become an integrated part of the phone.

The consumer gets this SD card through a banking relationship and inserts it into the phone *after* acquiring the phone. (Another version of this is the protective iPhone case from DeviceFidelity, with a secure memory card that hosts a contactless payment APP.) The bank can send the microSD card to the consumer to slot in the phone in much the same way that a GSM carrier provides a SIM card, the little plastic chip in every GSM phone globally that houses the phone subscriber identity, to the new subscriber to insert into the phone.

Two in five mobile device holders are active SD card users. In 2009, 90 percent of all shipped handsets that included memory cards used microSD card slots, making it the world-leading de facto interface of removable media. SD cards are becoming the dominant form factor. Even back in 2009, over 60 percent of all

mobile devices shipped included a microSD card slot.* However, it is still a clumsy round-hole-square-peg business model.

IN THE PHONE: If any party is an interested stakeholder in owning the mobile-shopper relationship, it is the wireless carrier. The wireless carrier has a vested interest in making sure that it is not removed from the equation by a side-loading memory chip shipped directly from your local bank. The carriers are advocating that the financial authentication should be enabled on the phone's SIM card, making them indispensable players in this new wallet game.

The wireless carriers are eyeing a new business model in which they magically load a bank card's credentials to the consumer's phone over the air. No muss, no fuss? The reality is that many of the business rules around this process have yet to be defined, and the bank community is leery of the carrier blocking it from the customer relationship and the potential bundled value-added services. The wireless carrier sees a business case for charging fees to service providers to manage their applications on the SIM card.

In the United Kingdom, Orange and T-Mobile have partnered to launch a payment service called Everything Everywhere, while AT&T (T-Mobile) and Verizon Wireless have set up a joint venture called Isis. France Telecom–Orange Group is aggressively rolling out a pan-Europe payment plan and trying to set up a global service for managing the provisioning of bank credentials to the phone. Key to the carriers' new business model is controlling the

*In 2007, the installed base of mobile device base with a microSD slot was over 50 percent. MicroSD slots are now standard on most smartphones. All form factors share the same interoperability and plug-and-play convenience. However, there are technical obstacles to using this chip as an NFC antenna. The MicroSD slots are often shielded under the phone battery and were not necessarily designed to transmit a wireless signal.

authentication of credentials to the phone (via the SIM). NFC authentication process is centered around a Trusted Service Manager (TSM). The TSM manages the provisioning of a device (secure element) for mobile payment. A TSM is the trusted party that communicates to the bank's and mobile phone's security systems.

Apple, Google, and the wireless carrier can become a TSM and coexist on the device. However, they can also compete. The carrier can be dispensable. Handset manufacturers can also enable payment credentials. Google is touting its Android singleTap shopping experience on the Android phone in partnership with financial institutions. CorFire, an SK telecom company, is selling white-label wallet solutions direct to retailers. Consumers can pay for an item using a credit card or gift card, redeem promotions, get offers, and earn loyalty points.

Google's small retail pilot programs in New York and San Francisco have generated considerable hype. The Citi MasterCard partnership allows the wallet to use PayPass's existing contactless network. At this point it is the only card accepted. As instructed by the website: "If you do not currently have a Citi MasterCard, you can apply for one here."

The world has changed (or is desperately trying to change). Across the value chain, all stakeholders are positioning and posturing. By some cosmic business alignment, on the same day, November 17, 2010, that Isis announced its m-wallet plans, Eric Schmidt, the CEO of Google, proclaimed the end of plastic payment. According to Mr. Schmidt, NFC-enabled phones with a digital wallet (or more specifically, a Google Wallet) will allow for universal payment and a host of other exhilarating actions. Soon.

There is no question that carriers and platform handset companies such as Google, Research in Motion (BlackBerry), and Apple

will be jousting over the next few years for control of their customers' mobile-payment credentials. The wireless carriers want the secure payment data stored on the devices' SIM cards, while the handset folk want to control this payment hub and accompanying lucrative value-added services such as tapping to open the car door or a consumer's confidential file data.

November 17 was surely a good public relations day, but did it finally signal the digital payment economy? Digital wallet, digital receipt, digital loyalty—perhaps it is still more market public relationship than a payment sea change. To move NFC commerce beyond wireless carrier, handset manufacturer, and financial services provider trials requires interoperability and global standards. It also demands ubiquitous reach at the store level.

The New Store

While it is difficult to see through the hype and excitement, there is clearly significant momentum. The appropriate standards to manage back-end systems NFC are achieving consistency and reliability in the mobile ecosystem at a store level. A not-for-profit association called GlobalPlatform is leading the charge in establishing and maintaining an interoperable and sustainable infrastructure for smart-card deployments. Its technology supports multi-application and multi-business model implementations, which delivers benefits to issuers, service providers, and technology suppliers.

Many banks have been reissuing their card portfolio with contactless cards. Visa is encouraging retailers to invest in contactless readers to allow shoppers to use internationally established contactless chip technology in their credit and debit cards (EMV). This unquestionably speeds up the infrastructure to allow for mobile

payments over the coming years. Large in-market trials are in place, and nearly every stakeholder in the value chain is discussing virtual cash and m-wallets. NFC is fast maturing, and we have graduated from "This is the year of mobile" to "This is the year of NFC."

If the industry in the late 1960s could muscle plastic card adoption, the powers that be should be up to the challenge of migrating the consumer toward NFCs in the early 2010s.

However, the store is a major barrier. There are still not enough RFID and NFC readers in retail to create a viable business in North America. Around 7 percent of merchant retail point of sale (PoS) is contactless enabled. While many discuss the need to invest in NFC technology in retail stores, there are not many stepping up to absorb the fees. While Visa may incentivize this migration, there are many cost considerations. Dave Talach, vice president of global product management at VeriFone, a payment terminal company, calls for subsidies for retailers to expand adoption of NFC in the store. VeriFone has backed this up with a commitment to retrofit its payment terminals. "The deployment and management of complex NFC technologies will require significant ongoing services from the retailer's payment systems provider," says Talach. "The costs of deploying and managing all of this new software should be borne by the new service provider who stands to gain the most. Retailers will not invest in good faith."

The shopper is oblivious to all these concerns. As a shopper, I need to be able to walk into any store and wave my mobile wallet. Ubiquitous reach may not be solved soon. At a Retail Industry Leaders Association (RILA) gathering in San Francisco, I took an informal vote with top retail executives on mobile marketing trends in their stores. There was a consensus in the room that mobile payment will be the main driver of mobile adoption. When the shop-

per's phone is connected with his wallet functionally, the shopper will more readily embrace other mobile services. Given this, will North American retailers embrace NFC in their stores soon?

Brian Parlotto, senior vice president of consumer products at InComm, says no. InComm is the industry-leading distributor of stored-value gift cards and prepaid products. The company processed over $13 billion in transactions in 2010. Parlotto is looking at InComm's technology road map. Mobile is key. He sees mobile *enhancing* but not changing existing payment and in-store processes. Mobile will allow for value-added virtual services to run on InComm's network.

"Of course, it seems as if NFC is around the corner," Parlotto says. "There is a lot of hype. The payment processors of the world have been pushing contactless payments for years. But if you look closer, there is little traction. US banking infrastructure is confusing for the consumer, with many hands in the process. Unlike Asian and European economies, the United States has hundreds of banks and payment processors.

"Look at mobile adoption in the United States," he continues. "It took over ten years to see SMS usage grow. This was with zero barriers to entry. Remember, the consumers already had the SMS services bundled on their phone, the networks had the back-end SMS infrastructure in place, and we have a clearly articulated business road map from Europe. NFC has none of this. Adoption will be slow."

You need mass adoption for technologies like NFC to fly, and both the shopper and the retailer are still waiting on the sidelines. Even with Google pushing its own NFC mobile wallet, there may not be enough incentive for retailers to put in the NFC readers, because while it speeds up a transaction, it doesn't make it any

cheaper for the shopkeeper. The reality is that plastic works for the retailer. Furthermore, mobile payment options will cost them to retrofit their hardware and may actually cost the retailer more on the transaction fees (charges levied per transaction for the acceptance of the card called an "interchange" fee) because of the card-non-present high-risk profile.

Interchange

Interchange is the fee paid between banks for the acceptance of a card-based transaction. Interchange fees have a complex pricing structure based on various factors, including the risk profile of the transaction (online, in-store, phone order, whether the card is present for the transaction, and so forth). Mobile transactions may lead to higher interchange fees, which would discourage retailers from embracing this payment type until the shopper demands it.

Will the store continue to be the obstacle? "I will say this," explains Tom Purves, business leader of product innovation at Visa. "History tells us merchants will be reluctant to adopt any new payment scheme if it introduces any sort of new costs—be they one-time costs or interchange—unless it directly helps them grow their sales or reduce costs in other areas."

But this is not always the case. Purves offers an example: "Look at taxi drivers in New York City. They were at first reluctant to adopt contactless payments. Now, however, they love accepting Visa payWave transactions, as they've discovered the same customers are giving much higher tips.

"Merchants tend to avidly adopt new payment methods when it helps them reach new customers, grow average spend of existing customers, and/or enable entirely new business models."

The New Wallets

Everyone in the NFC value chain is posturing. There are many parties interested in advancing and capitalizing on the mobile payment channel and becoming the new shopper wallet—while attempting to mobilize and possibly eliminate billions of plastic cards.

One of the chief reasons that it is difficult to get the financial services providers, retailers, phone manufacturers, wireless carriers, and PoS operators all to play nice in the sandbox is the question of ownership. Who owns the consumer's m-wallet?

In August 2011, Ogilvy & Mather conducted a study asking would-be mobile payment consumers what mobile payment companies they would most likely trust. Incumbent vendors such as Visa, MasterCard, American Express, and PayPal topped the list.

- Visa 39.6%
- MasterCard 35.9%
- American Express 35.8%
- PayPal 34.3%
- Apple 22.9%
- Google 19.5%
- Facebook 12.1%

Consumers may feel safer with payment pure-play companies that do not have mixed revenue goals that may include marketing, advertising, or simply selling more devices. Often, however, it is sleight of hand, and it is difficult to separate pure payment from overlapping lines of business: American Express is working with Facebook to provide cardholder coupons; Mastercard is side by side with Google Offers in the new Android wallet. Perhaps

Ogilvy's survey respondents are identifying the companies they trust to be *front facing* in the m-wallet relationship?

"There are only a few companies that have the muscle to enter the mobile payment market," says Keith Sibson, vice president of product for NetSpend, a prepaid card company. "It takes time to develop a trusted relationship with a larger consumer base. Established digital-payment companies are best positioned to dominate: Amazon.com, PayPal, and Apple have spent years tethering payment information to shopper accounts, which puts them at an advantage over payments start-ups. Newcomers will struggle to make progress with tethered payments because they have to overcome the friction of setup."

While the Google Wallet, CorFire, and others work to tackle the unwieldy store cash register, perhaps look to Apple for the first successful NFC payment network. More impressive than Apple's design innovation is the company's ability to develop a smart central consumer wallet. Its iTunes investment may pay off (again). If NFC needs a payment home, the iTunes retail store may be the first success story. With zero barriers, Apple could allow consumers to tap and check out on iTunes off smart magazines, smart posters, or other smart products all marked with RFID tags.

Apple is in an interesting position in the near term. The largest wallet subscriber base will win, and Apple is farther ahead than banks or wireless carriers in linking an open wallet to a phone account. It has tethered its payment system to 400 million credit cards, giving it ten times the APP purchase volume as Android. With iTunes, the "pickup" is already completed, and purchases are frictionless. By contrast, Google's focus on the retail point of sale may inhibit growth.

However, Apple's present business model is built for digital and virtual goods, requiring a payout of 30 percent per transaction. A 30 percent fee will allow only for high-margin digital goods in the Apple stores. Unless Apple reduces the "merchant discount" fee to single digits, to compete with traditional credit and debit cards, it will not expand its reach into physical retail.

There may be a middle ground, as business models are changing daily in the mobile industry. Apple, as an NFC latecomer, has an opportunity to take far away from the retail PoS. With minimal barriers Apple could allow consumers to TAP on smart magazines, smart posters, smart products all tagged with RFID tags and check out in the iTunes cloud. Merchants and brands may pay higher fees for the convenience of frictionless payment, but double-digit fees are unlikely to be accepted. Apple, Android, PayPal, and Amazon. com will continue to be the leading virtual payment vendors until the retailers can connect the NFC dots end to end and the banks' new NFC phone wallets have a rival subscriber base. Until then, we will not see mass consumer adoption.

Let's revisit our payment chart from page 39 and add NFC payments:

Goods	Type	Transport	Funding
• Horoscope	• Digital	• SMS	• Carrier Bill
• Web Access	• Virtual	• WAP Billing	• Carrier Bill
• Game APP	• Digital	• APP Store	• Credit Card
• Subway Ticket	• Virtual	• NFC / PoE	• Stored Value
• Shoes	• Physical	• NFC / PoS	• Credit / Debit

Quick-Checkout Wallet:
Nearer Than Near Field

Driving along the freeway from Sybase's head office outside San Francisco with Cameron Franks, area vice president of America's sales at Sybase, a global messaging and mobile-commerce provider, we spent the journey discussing the media focus on NFC.

"The industry fixates too much on a particular technology solution, when it should be focused on the end result," explained Franks. "Much-hyped retail and banking solutions such as NFC are simply a channel to drive transactions. Whether we use this or simple SMS for banking, the goal is to drive consumers to use their m-wallet and spend, transact more.

"This is like asking, 'Do consumers need technologies like LTE or WiMAX?'" he continued, referring to long-term evolution networks and worldwide interoperability for microwave access, respectively. "The consumer does not care. They need faster mobile broadband; they don't care how technology delivers it. Near field communication is a radio-frequency standard, not a consumer-facing payment type. What consumers really need is more convenient ways of making payments."

There are seven radios in your smart phone, combined with half a dozen other sensors, not to mention a really good web browser and thriving APP markets. We as an industry really could be using any or all of these options to create new, convenient forms of payment or new, richer retail shopping experiences. Franks and many others are solution agnostics. They advocate whatever will work to drive more transactions and more commerce. The focus should be on driving mobile payments, not fixating on solving proximity payment at the point of sale.

Franks added, "I understand the value of NFC phones for parking and daily transit fees that provide the added benefit of reminders and automatically extend payment when time is running out on the meter. This is ideal for speed through turnstiles and transactions, and utilization can be driven by pricing, as London Transport does with Oyster on the contactless card side." But beyond this, Franks seemed to struggle to see the user benefit or which industry will see significant uptake. "The convenience factor of tapping a phone versus swiping a card—outside of mass transit—is not significant enough to change user behavior, so I remain somewhat dubious about widespread adoption."

It is all about eliminating friction for the would-be shopper. David Dorf, lead PoS engineer at Oracle in Austin, Texas, measured the NFC transaction and questions whether the consumer may abandon this channel at the point of purchase. There was a delay of two seconds per transaction file. With multiple files, this could lead to frustration. And this involves merely *reading* data—what if we need to write to the phone, or send coupons and perform other actions? "Moving the phone away from the reader during a write operation can cause an error," notes Dorf. "When a coupon is redeemed, we may want to erase it or add a new one during checkout. This extends the time even longer." The devil is in the details.

Until the tap-and-go mobile wallet is frictionless, and ubiquitous, inspiring confidence and driving revenue, there are effective commerce applications that do not ask for any relationship up front but ask only at the mobile point of decision. In the first stumbling years of the 2010s, the NFC payment channel does not have the consumer reach, particularly in markets such as the United States.

Some exceptions include Japan's operators, which have established a transaction model and have entered the banking market; and the Philippines, where mobile money transfer has satisfied a need for low-cost remittance transfer to an expatriate community outside of the country.

Once the phone is purchased and in the consumer's pocket, it is a challenge to motivate her to add any additional service manually. Consumer inertia sets in. So if the merchant does not have the luxury of having an onboard billing agreement with the consumer or leveraging bundled bank-activated NFC chips, how do we start a commerce relationship?

Financial services providers find it very challenging to coax the consumer to sign up for a payment service (m-wallet) because the shopper needs to invest time and effort to tether to the phone for some future convenience. These hurdles to activate or sticker a phone are stifling adoption. In addition, retailers are not ready to invest in new payment terminals based on future demand.

How Do You Snag a Surfer?

If we look to another industry that is debating how to pop the commerce question—namely, the large-screen Internet—we see the same inertia. There is a heated debate presently on how and when to ask the consumer to pay for online content, as ad dollars alone are not enough to fund premium online content, according to keynote presentations at the Interactive Advertising Bureau (IAB) annual general meeting. Industry pundits are discussing establishing a payment coalition that would sell a web paypass. Each page view would have a click toll. Many are leery to copy the pay-wall model pioneered by the *Wall Street Journal,* out of concern that popping the commerce question too aggressively will alienate the surfing consumer.

With the increasing number of premium pay walls that are now popping up, I cannot believe that a consumer will bother to sign up for multiple sites. (It is the same problem we have in mobile with multiple APPS—only five are really used.) I strongly believe that the *New York Times, WSJ,* and others should join hands and work with a neutral body like the IAB to create a universal key for a premium-content consortium (consising of multiple premium publishers) and the pay key is then metered out based on page visits to member sites. IAB makes a few pennies, and the publishers get cashing: one-stop shopping for web surfers that want rich content. We need to resolve this online before we rinse and repeat on mobile. To fill a void, Apple seems to be rising to this challenge with its subscription APP model. Who will resolve this on the mobile web?

If we draw out a matrix of (1) online billing versus (2) mobile and credit card billing versus (3) carrier billing companies, Fandango, Adgregate Markets, Billing Revolution, and others like them reside in a quadrant of their own. This category becomes more frictionless as end-to-end commerce takes place on the phone.

So how does the bank or m-wallet convince the coy mobile consumer to tether his or her billing account to the phone number?

When is the right time to pop the commerce question to the shopper: "Credit card details, please?"

If we do not have the ability to bill the phone account, when do we gather account information? Do we ask the consumer for credit card details up front and interrupt the sale, or do we wait until we have her engaged in a mobile CRM channel and then ask the dirty question?

Existing commerce payment wallets such as Amazon.com and Apple require a formal sign-up with tethered billing information before a hint of commerce has been performed. This is not a native mobile checkout. The commerce muscle of Apple and Amazon .com allow them to acquire a mobile-commerce relationship online *before* a purchase begins on the phone. When you have this stored payment information, selling books is a small step removed from selling DVD players and toasters. It took Amazon.com six years to realize that it is not the content but the m-commerce channel that is the central value proposition.

However, even though mobile phone sales outnumber personal computer sales, mobile accounts for only 5 percent of digital commerce. To drive conversion, these payment portals may need to make the checkout process more impulsive and native to the phone.

Pizza Commerce

Quick service restaurants (QSR), or fast food, are the poster children for impulse "I am hungry" commerce. The industry grew out of the post–World War I automobile boom servicing the urban consumer on the go. The industry was optimized to exit the customer as fast and as full as possible. To do this, the menu was

simplified, cooking was streamlined, and packaging and payment were stripped down to a fine American art form. White Castle, as the prototypal fast-food chain, opened in Wichita, Kansas, in 1916, introducing the limited-menu, high-volume, low-cost, high-speed hamburger restaurant.

Mobile-commerce folk need to look to the speed and efficiencies tailored to the mobile drive-through American and understand the following: online, thoughtful commerce is to mobile impulse commerce what slow dining is to fast food. Mobile commerce is "pizza commerce," stripped of option paralysis and optimized for one-click decision making.

- Targeted offers
- Limited aisle (limited menu)
- Single-click exit

Because of this strategy and allocation of resources, the pizza chains Pizza Hut and Papa John's seem to wield the same commerce muscle as Amazon.com and Apple. They have successfully managed to run mobile services that require online pre-purchase setup. Most orders are made simply by clicking on a preset favorite or triggering the "last order."

Eliminating option and location paralysis equals millions of dollars in mobile pizza purchases.

Impromptu, Intimate Decisions

Leery of clicking on an advertisement on a mobile website? What if it were a major movie or game release, and you could click to buy, or maybe even preorder a bonus gift for shopping early? If

the carrot is compelling, the shopper may click. But what then? How do we close the sale before the shopper abandons this whim and returns to surf content or simply closes the phone and continues with her mobile day.

Henry Wong, CEO of Adgregate Markets, launched a shopper ad campaign for the DVD release of the movie *Inglourious Basterds*. Consumers could preorder the DVD on their mobile phones. The commerce happened directly in the advertisement, without "clicking out" to another m-commerce application or storefront. The campaign demonstrated that between equivalent online ads and the mobile ads, mobile closed transactions at a higher rate.

Moreover, while mobile shoppers abandoned their carts at a slightly higher rate than the online shoppers, the intent to purchase was three times higher than the response from those with PCs. Wong was surprised because, in spite of the smaller form factor of the keyboard for mobile checkout, mobile was far superior at capitalizing on the impulse nature of the shopper than online media. This is especially remarkable, he notes, "when you

consider that online shopping carts have had a twenty-year head start in optimizing the checkout and cart process. Capitalizing on convenient, on-the-go mobile purchasing was a key driver in this campaign."

Why did this work despite all the obstacles thrown at the mobile shopper? Was it the entertainment media, which is a close relative of the impulse ringtone? The "Want it! Need it!" mentality of the target eighteen- to twenty-four-year-old male demographic?

"The goal," Wong explains, "was to generate impromptu purchases. Allowing in-banner purchase worked because the billing option was presented at point of inspiration." Immediacy and convenience seem to be the two factors that work for ringtones and now work for DVD sales.

"Want it! Need it!" works only if the messaging has bull's-eye targeting. Adgregate worked with the Jumptap ad network, which can pull detailed consumer information (anonymously) directly from certain carriers' records. Targeting drives clicks. Targeting drives conversion.

Whether this is targeted entertainment content or targeted consumer product, shoppers will respond in-channel only if they feel there is a unique one-to-one dialogue. Take Procter & Gamble's mobile direct-to-consumer (D2C) sale of Always feminine hygiene products. P&G, like many brands, is trying to establish a direct relationship with the shopper outside of the store. It is genius to start with intimate products that many shoppers do not necessarily want piled on top of their shopping cart. The Always Me mobile APP provides information on the woman's menstrual period and cycle; enables her to submit private, personal questions to a health professional; and allows the mobile shopper to purchase the product discreetly on the phone via a Shop Always button.

But "Want it! Need it!" goes only so far. The clumsy process of entering your credit card information is a huge impediment. We know we can do this online, but what is the native mobile solution for the "impromptu purchase"? Is it a universal wallet solution?

"You do not want to force the mobile user to visit a website to register. This interrupts and terminates the transaction," says Andy Kleitsch, CEO of Billing Revolution. However, companies in this commerce category are going one step further by allowing the consumer to tether her card permanently. Enter billing information once, and the consumer can now click to buy with *no* PIN and *no* password. The billing information and permission are tethered to the phone number.

So, This Is Love in the Interim

Companies like Visa are aggressively launching a digital wallet (a one-click shopping solution), substituting an onerous log-in with a simple alias and password optimized for the impulse shopper. Visa acquired PlaySpan, a payment marketplace that allows for quick checkout for games and virtual goods, enabling players to purchase in-game items without disrupting game play. Visa is using this architecture to build a quick checkout platform for all digital screens.

Like PayPal's core business that has allowed the company to dominate PC-based checkout, capturing 18 percent of payment globally, Visa is creating a simple process of tethering credit information to the phone, allowing its consumers to check out in the internet cloud. In doing this, Visa bypasses all the pain of NFC devices, in-store hardware, and chip *accreditation*.

Let's revisit our payment chart (pages 39 and 57) yet again and this time add tethered payments:

Goods	Type	Transport	Funding
• Horoscope	• Digital	• SMS	• Carrier Bill
• Web Access	• Virtual	• WAP Billing	• Carrier Bill
• Game APP	• Digital	• APP Store	• Credit Card
• Subway Ticket	• Virtual	• NFC	• Stored Value
• Shoes	• Physical	• NFC / PoS	• Credit / Debit
• Coupon	• Virtual	• QR Code	• Stored Value
• Shoes	• Physical	• MWeb Online Checkout*	• Credit Card
• Shoes	• Physical	• MWeb Singleclick†	• Credit Card

It is clear in the 2010s that we can include physical goods in our checkout options and that the retail question has moved from "What's in *your* wallet?" to "What *is* your wallet?" The retailer and shopper know that the very fiber of the transaction is changing. However, whatever approach you take to incentivize, entice, or goad shoppers into mobile transactions, be ever mindful not to try to "educate" the shopper on a new service. The shopper will adopt or reject a service based on utility and convenience. It is pure hubris and not good business practice to presume that shoppers need to be trained. Just try to identify what mobile behavior your consumers are using outside your stores and adapt this behavior into your retail services. For the last word, let's look to Coca-Cola, the largest single seller of product in the United States. Doug Busk, head of the company's global mobile strategy, ends all his presentations with a snapshot taken of a roadside diner tabletop. Under this photograph is a caption that reads: "A Coke, a phone, and some cash. A beautiful picture, indeed. ☺" "It is not the mode that matters," says Busk. "SMS works. As will credit card, NFC . . ."

* Mobile web checkout that emulates online checkout.

† Mobile web checkout that simplifies checkout for a native mobile impulse purchase.

Whatever mobile wallet the consumer decides to adopt and use to connect phone, cash, and product purchase is the right wallet.

Security: The Elephant in the Room

At a DefCon Kids event in Vegas in 2011, a ten-year-old hacker going by the handle of CyFi explained that by advancing the clock on a tablet or phone she could speed up the pace of life-cycle games like Farmville. By disconnecting the phone from the network and advancing the device clock only by small increments, CyFi could fool the game clock into growing instant pumpkins.

Whether you are hacking seasons in Farmville or tackling more insidious payment fraud, there will be inevitable vulnerabilities. Such code oversights are often exploited to allow attackers to run their own code and access confidential client data. Is this the elephant in the room? Is mobile commerce fraught with security concerns? We know that new payment channels are not immune to mobile fraudsters. Jimmy Shah, mobile security researcher at McAfee Labs, pointed out in a blog post* that Google Wallet can be reverse engineered so that a fraudster could possibly get access to its "secure element" and ultimately create a malicious application that emulates the official payment APP, fooling the secure element chip into giving up the shopper's credentials.

Can you say "phishing and phreaking a phone" three times fast?

According to a 2010 report from Juniper Networks, an industry research company,† "More than 76% of consumers surveyed use

* http://blogs.mcafee.com/enterprise/mobile/looking-into-google-wallets-security-setup.

† www.juniper.com.lv/uk/en/company/press-center/press-releases/2010/pr_2010_10_26-11_00.html.

their smartphones or tablets to access sensitive personal or business information, including: 51% to enter or modify passwords; 43% to access banking or credit card statements; 30% to access utility bills; 20% to share financial information such as credit card numbers; 18% to access employer's proprietary information; 17% to access medical records; and 16% to share social security numbers."

Is the media simply scaremongering? Dave Talach from Veri-Fone slams industry scare tactics around new mobile wallets.* There is hype, and it is understandable that NFC security naysayers unsettle Talach. But unfortunately, we need to get ready for a turbulent ride. Whether the phone is more secure than your cowhide wallet is not the point. Consumers are irrational folk and will adopt or reject a technology based on criteria that are not purely technological and surely not always logical.

Any security breach of the shopper and his or her shopping experience is a breach of trust, and mobile trust is sacrosanct. The phone is a particularly intimate device because it stores private addresses, secret texts, family photos, and perhaps their accompanying health card and social security number. The phone, unlike the cowhide wallet, is an extension of one's identity.

Try This

In a large crowd, ask each person to pass his or her phone to the person on the left. Once the uncomfortable murmur settles, ask them to continue passing each phone to the person to their left. A three-seat distance from your personal device creates unnatural separation anxiety.

* www.mobilewaytopay.com/2011/05/09/tin-foil-wallets-and-other-scare-tactics-of-nfc-progress.

According to AT&T, a consumer who loses a mobile phone notifies the carrier within just twenty-five minutes, on average, whereas according to First Data, it takes the average person up to twenty-four hours to realize that she has lost her wallet.

How Long Has It Been Since You've Looked at Your Mobile Phone (to Check the Time, to Check for/Respond to Messages or Calls, Etc.)?

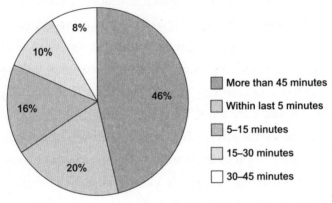

Source: InsightExpress's Mobile Consumer Research, July 2010

To address the fear of hacking, Google tries to explain to the shopper that the payment encryption (secure element) is separate from the phone's memory. In the "How It Works" section of the Google Wallet website, Google writes, "Think of the Secure Element as a *separate computer*, capable of running programs and storing data."

But with private data such as location, profile, and banking information floating through the cloud, there is sure to be multiple security abuses. The reality is that until there is mass mobile-commerce adoption, neither hackers nor security police will focus on mobile.

There are always going to be vulnerabilities, and mobile-payment folk need to know that they have to balance the risk. Fraudsters have continually been able to thwart security measures. In the face of this, banks have shown that they have strong stomachs for payment risk on new platforms. Ralph Poore, chief cryptologist at Cryptographic Assurance Services, a data security consulting company, maps what he refers to as the "evolution of risk":

Risk was relatively low when cash was handed over the counter at the local bank branch. As banks expanded their reach electronically, they needed to develop processes to deal with vulnerabilities in the network. ATMs needed to accommodate *teller-not-present* transactions. Catalogue phone orders needed to accommodate *card-not-present* transactions. As remote payment access moved online and now into the wireless space, with third-party operating systems and third-party applications, risk and vulnerabilities increased— not only for the shopper but for the entire payment value chain.

Early in 2011, Mobile Marketer published a story titled "How to Compromise the Starbucks Rewards Card APP in 90 Seconds." The Starbucks mobile stored-value program mirrored the functionality of the Starbucks plastic stored-value card. Instead of swiping the card, the attendant scans the number off the phone via a 2-D code. To compromise the system, the forger could simply photo capture a Starbucks 2-D code off an unattended phone and proceed to debit the owner's prepaid account at any Starbucks café.

What is interesting about this scenario is not the fraud. Plastic stored-value Starbucks cards are stolen, lost, or misused every day.

What is of note is that the mobile misdemeanor gets more press. Virtual payment is under more scrutiny, possibly because we have such high expectations for this new channel. What will help the industry advance mobile payments?

We all know that encrypted digital communications provide the highest security. Still, there are huge vulnerabilities. A recent study by the nonprofit consumer education and advocacy organization Privacy Rights Clearinghouse* indicated (hold your breath) that wireless carriers *turn off encryption* on voice and data in order to optimize data speeds, as encryption slows down the network. Few US carriers encrypt digital transmissions, in contrast to Europe. However, this may be a moot point: several studies have shown that the GSM encryption and authentication algorithms and protocols are vulnerable to cryptanalysis in real time using commercially available technology. In response to this risk, X9.org is developing Wireless Management and Security standards. Additionally, X9 and MEF (www.mefmobile.org) are working on best practices for mobile-commerce security.

The industry seriously needs to look at developing and improving security standards immediately. In order for shoppers to feel comfortable with new technology, they have to be confident in the security of the device.

A Call for Confidence

Keith Enright, Google's chief privacy officer, is one of the few voices openly discussing mobile consumer-information risk management.

* Privacy Rights Clearinghouse/UCAN: Fact Sheet 2: Wireless Communications: Voice and Data Privacy: www.privacyrights.org/fs/fs2-wire.htm.

"The mobile channel and mobile payment mechanisms can be secured, like any other channel," he says. "Not perfectly, but relative to risk. However, questioning whether mobile security is the same as or different than online security misses the point."

For Enright, digital security is the ability to establish effective controls based on a thorough understanding of the strengths and vulnerabilities of the system. "The analysis online or in a mobile environment would be similar, but the most effective controls may *differ.*" So what are these "effective controls," and how do we know we are doing a good job addressing the vulnerabilities of the mobile channel?

"The mobile and payment channels are similar in that they are both bolted on to groups of underlying technologies that are changing very quickly," he continues, "just as the World Wide Web evolved far past the goals of its conception. Uses and applications of mobile technology are outpacing effective controls to mitigate known and anticipated risks. With this in mind, the mobile industry could benefit from collaborative efforts to take existing, well-established security risk assessment methodologies and standards, adapt them as appropriate, and apply them consistently to new and expanded uses of mobile technology."

Technology innovation is outgunning the speed of effective controls. Pairing location and commerce, for example, challenges existing security and privacy controls. Location-based services are one of many mobile anomalies that make this channel unique.

Like Enright, the folk at Dell see m-security as a superset of electronic commerce standards. We cannot replicate online security standards to mobile. Not all compliance standards (like the Payment Card Industry's Data Security Standard, or PCI DSS) fully address mobile transactions. So what m-commerce standards

need to be adopted to protect the confidentiality, integrity, and availability of customer data?

Sourav Dutt's security team at Dell in Round Rock, Texas, believes that mobile devices require special considerations such as the security of network technology's accessibility to unencrypted locally stored data, ease of targeted attacks, reduction in the complexity of successful fraud/phishing attempts, and a generally more broad attack surface.

Simple words of advice:

1. Do not make mobile security an add-on. Involve security in every stage of the m-commerce application-development life cycle, including planning, design, development, testing, retesting, re-retesting, release, and post-release.

2. Educate developers and testers on different aspects of m-commerce application security.

3. Practice due diligence in researching different areas of security (including mobile device attack vectors) in order to accurately perform a security audit of m-commerce applications.

We Went Through This All Before

Didn't we go through this same dance with online security? There have been several grandiose schemes to make Internet payments more secure, but today it pretty much boils down to using two encryption keys: SSL (Secure Socket Layer) and RSA (which stands for the encrypytion authors: Rivest, Shamir, and Adleman). We know that no security system is invulnerable and impervious to a superhacker. But we developed the Payment Card Industry's Data

Security Standard (PCI DSS) that is now used as a retail industry standard to manage shopper payment data to ward off legislative action. PCI has not begun to look at mobile payment. Its plate is fairly full as it is.

The very fact that we are considering tethering a personal device with an RFID tag to track payment presents big question marks for anyone concerned about security and privacy. Can an individual be tracked by phone tag if a powerful scanner is used for nefarious reasons? Quite possibly, says cryptologist Ralph Poore. "If I have a passive key in my phone that can identify my bank information with a wave of my phone, what is to stop someone from tracking me when I am not waving the phone?" According to Poore, shopper intent is key to security. The shopper that needs to intentionally *start* doing something and then *stop* doing something in order to activate a transaction is more secure.

Miller Abel, standards architect at Microsoft, calls this a red herring. "There are a few erroneous things we've seen reported that are fueling an unsettling but ambiguous sense of security risk," he says. This brings to mind the hypothetical situation of a scammer bumping someone on a subway train, who "sniffs" sensitive information from the target's phone, allowing him to encode a plastic credit card that would allow him to fraudulently buy a sweater in a retail or online store. "That's just BS," scoffs Abel. "Capturing information is not by itself a security threat. If there is no exploit, there is no fraud."

Abel says that the confidentiality of wireless transmission over these RFID tags using near field communication (NFC) is a moot issue. Many of the contactless payment cards use encrypted exchanges between the smartcard and the cash register and will communicate only with a suitably credentialed hardware security

module. Eavesdropping on that conversation would not yield anything exploitable.

"We should also remember," Abel adds, "that there are at least three forms of risk management for card payments that do not depend on the security of the wireless link: in the smartcard, card risk management; in the point of sale, terminal risk management; and in the payment network, payment risk management. Issuing and acquiring banks also manage settlement and clearance risk, currency risk, and other risks."

The industry is so nascent that banks have not resolved whether mobile security measures applied to the phone will allow for these fast-checkout or contactless transactions to be called "card-present" as opposed to the higher-risk "card-not-present" nomenclature. The implications are profound to the retailer and the shopper.

As the industry tries to understand the opportunity and the risks, some retail executives are sounding the alarm. "There are going to be some symbolic lynchings of a few m-commerce players by regulators before we settle on best practices in this space," cautioned one retail privacy executive. Whether this is fueled by real or hyped security concerns, we are in uncharted territory. Remote payment, linking payment, and location all have unforeseen effects on privacy and security. 2011 was a novelty. As the tonnage in the mobile basket increases, there will be more oversight and scrutiny.

Whether the concern is exaggerated or valid, the biggest challenge for this nascent industry is building consumer confidence in the channel. According to research from the management consulting and technology services company Accenture, 45 percent of mobile shoppers would like to pay via their phone; however, 73 percent have significant privacy and theft concerns. The United

States and Europe lag dramatically behind Asia, Africa, and Latin America in positively embracing mobile payment.

Trust is important across all retail touch points. Bryan Gailey and Alan Treadgold, retail experts at the ARC Worldwide agency, surveyed shoppers about what matters most to them.* As you can see, trust outgunned service, value, return policy, and price.

What Was Most Important?

- Convenient location61 percent
- Store I can trust. .59 percent
- Great selection of products.59 percent
- Has good value for the money55 percent
- Has a consistent online and in-store
 return policy .54 percent
- Makes shopping quick and easy53 percent
- Prompt service .52 percent
- Keeps prices lower than the competition . . .52 percent

To build confidence, the retail and banking community cannot wait for legislation to mandate security standards. X9.org, the financial standards body that brought us online PCI compliance standards, has announced that it is currently working on mobile-commerce standards—this is good.

It is the Internet all over again. And mobile should not wait for the same Beltway drums.

* © 2011 Leo Burnett and Arc Worldwide.

4 MOBILE COMMERCE: NO ONE'S HOME

Before we plod down the list of viable m-commerce channels, let's disabuse some in-market notions. Some touted solutions may not be ready for prime-time commerce, either lacking the necessary install base to succeed or being "use proof"—that is, hiding behind too many clicks.

The would-be mobile marketing manager servicing the brand, retailer, or content owner needs to accept the tiresome reality that however exciting a mobile solution may be, the ultimate goal is to drive reach, frequency, and conversion. The mobile buy needs return on advertising (ROA), and the mobile strategy needs to provide return on investment (ROI).

As most of the brands and retailers evaluating mobile commerce options are *not* mobile companies, it is *not* their role to innovate or to incur any risk. They need mobile to help make their traditional media work harder, *or* connect media dots that historically they could not connect without mobile, *or* engage with the consumer in places they want to engage with a mobile channel. The brand or retailer needs to identify what is working with the

consumer and follow suit. It is important to identify what is ready for prime time and avoid the rabbit holes.

Mobile Hype

"The challenge is navigating the hype," says James Crawford, executive director of the Global Retail Executive Council (GREC). "It is easy to come up with great ideas. For example, in the case of m-coupons, ninety percent of retailers cannot or do not support them. Retailers may have historically missed the trend by decades, but remember, retail is all about mainstream adoption. It is possible for a solution vender to innovate in one store or in one enterprise loop. However, the CPG (consumer packaged goods company) needs universal adoption across major stores.

"In many cases, we can expect mobile innovation to follow Gartner, an industry reseach company's, 'Hype Cycle.' Retailers and brands get excited about a new solution. There is hype, then when the solution does not immediately deliver results, it crashes, disappears, and then grows slowly, reemerging over a longer period of time," explains Crawford.

Gartner's Hype Cycle, introduced in 1995, characterizes the typical progression of an emerging technology, from overenthusiasm through a period of disillusionment to an eventual understanding of the technology's relevance and role in a market or domain. The time frame from the technology trigger to the stable use of a given in-market solution is upward of ten years. Let's not kid ourselves: we are still on the mobile roller coaster between high expectations and low return.

Mobile is a model of Gartner's Hype Cycle. The typical cycle, or what Gartner refers to as the "raw" cycle, falls into the following phases:

- **TECHNOLOGY TRIGGER**: The Hype Cycle starts when a breakthrough occurs, accompanied by a public demonstration of technology innovation. Increasingly, people hear of its potential, and a wave of "buzz" quickly builds as everyone wants to be the first to pass on the news. Mobile is sold to brands and retailers by early technology evangelists.
- **PEAK OF INFLATED EXPECTATIONS**: Early adopters that like to be ahead of the curve seek out the technology and jump on it before their competitors. The suppliers of the technology boast about their early prestigious customers, and other companies want to join in so they aren't left behind. A bandwagon effect kicks in, and the technology is pushed to its limits as companies try it out in a range of settings. At this point, the technology is viewed as a panacea, with little regard to its suitability for each application.
- **TROUGH OF DISILLUSIONMENT**: As time passes, impatience for results begins to replace the original excitement about potential value. The same few stories of early success have been re-

peated over and over, but now a deeper look often shows those same companies still struggling to derive meaningful value. Problems with performance, slower-than-expected adoption, or failure to deliver financial returns in the time anticipated all lead to missed expectations. Many of these failures center on inappropriate uses of the technology. Less favorable stories start to emerge as most companies realize things aren't as easy as they first seemed. The media, always needing a new angle to keep readers interested, switches to featuring the challenges rather than the opportunities of the technology.

- **SLOPE OF ENLIGHTENMENT**: Some early adopters overcome the initial hurdles, begin to experience benefits, see the proverbial light at the end of the tunnel, and recommit efforts to move forward. Drawing on the experience of early adopters, understanding grows about where the technology can be used to good effect and, just as important, where it brings little or no value. Over time, the technology matures as suppliers improve products based on early feedback. Methodologies for applying it successfully are codified, and best practices for its use are communicated.

- **PLATEAU OF PRODUCTIVITY**: With the real-world benefits of the technology demonstrated and accepted, growing numbers of organizations feel comfortable with the now greatly reduced levels of risk. A sharp uptick ("hockey stick") in adoption begins, and penetration accelerates rapidly as a result of productive and useful value.

The challenge is that "mobile" is such an all-encompassing technology category. Each mobile solution has its own X/Y axis point on the following chart. One technology may have success-

fully moved through to the plateau of productivity; however, other newer solutions may only be the first leg of inflated expectations.

Here is my mobile "super" hype chart:

This mismatch causes an additional complexity across the ecosystem. Mature "mobile" solutions such as messaging are in the "plateau of productivity" cycle while nascent "mobile" solutions such as NFC are in the "technology trigger" cycle. Mobile is a big word and solutions vendors are all using the same vernacular. A retailer or brand may talk about developing a "mobile strategy" and latch onto one particular mobile solution, possibly thinking that it is already established as a productive and useful tool. It is no surprise that there are so many mobile adopters hitting troughs.

"I have run that cycle in the online space, and we are now in that phase with mobile," says Michael Cooper, vice president of HomeDepot.com. "But you have to innovate. Just need to make sure that there is a balancing act between innovating and knowing when to shut things down. In the digital business, you can throw away money fast. You have to oscillate between exploring new ideas and throwing out strategies that are not working."

For months, Cooper had been meeting with various players in the mobile value chain, discussing how best to leverage mobile both now and down the road. When we met, he had just returned from a meeting with Jim Balsillie, co-CEO of RIM, maker of the BlackBerry. "I am in the process of asking questions," said Cooper.

What is more dangerous for Michael than following the hype is becoming blinded by his own preconceptions of the media and his shoppers' behavior. "I am wary of my own paradigms; of seeing the world based on the way that I personally use mobile," he says. "You have to ask questions. You have to be open to innovation. That is how you grow your business."

Sir Martin Sorrell, CEO of the WPP, a large agency conglomerate, has said that mobile is the most "overhyped medium in the short term" and the most "underhyped medium in the long term." Here are three hype areas to explore with caution in the short term.

Japan and 2-D Bar Code Myth Busting

As a delinquent youth, I spent many years in Japan as part of the Stanford University Asia program. When I graduated, I got a dream job working for Dentsu, a Japanese media giant, translating and running errands on Madonna's 1990 Blonde Ambition world tour.

I wish I could tell you that I studied hard or that I learned all the ins and outs of Japan's mobile economy. On both counts, I failed. I spent my time at a bar near my office at Dentsu, Eizo Jigyo Kyoku,* in the Tsukiji fish market, or touring the country on my 250cc Kawasaki, and I totally missed Japan's mobile revolution.

Japan was Pre-Mobile. There was no Internet, no PC install

*Dentsu Film Distribution Division.

base in the Japanese home, and no mobile communication. We all know that with the introduction of Nippon Telegraph & Telephone Corp.'s iMode service, there was an unprecedented adoption of mobile devices in Japan and a technology leapfrog phenomenon over PC web to mobile web.

Dan Rosen, head of mobile for AKQA, the world's largest independent digital agency, calls Japan the "mobile mother ship." It has unquestionably led the charge. But look long and hard, and there are many mobile urban legends.

When I returned to Japan in 2005 to do business in the mobile space, I met with NTT. Dr. Yasu Nakamura, one of the chief engineers at the telecom, was my host. When I was ushered into the NTT "Wireless World of the Future" presentation and given a chance to wand my NTT phone over a vending machine (to dispense a can of Coke) and over an arcade game (for a chance to hook a Hello Kitty doll), I asked Dr. Nakamura why Japan was the only country in the world where SMS was not used as a primary communication channel. I was confused, because DoCoMo's e-mail allowed for (slow) peer-to-peer communication, but there was no instant brand-activation or impulse-purchase channel.

Dr. Nakamura showed me the (then) nascent 2-D bar code reader solution, which allowed for brand activation. In trials, 2-D codes were placed on products, and a prebundled phone reader allowed this code to launch a mobile web page with product details. McDonald's was slapping it on burgers to activate promotions. Some Japanese brands were using these codes to link to product and diet informa-

tion. DoCoMo employees proudly used it on their business cards to link to corporate information.

Killer SMS

I explained that linking anonymously to a webpage is a powerful discovery tool, but it does not allow for a one-to-one relationship with the brand. I tried to sell Dr. Nakamura on the virtues of SMS as a brand channel with no luck. I even ran off to meet with the Chiba Lotte Marines baseball team and Coca-Cola Japan to convince them to buy in to a trial, but Dr. Nakamura indicated that the SMS for which I was lobbying had been shut down, and there would be no resurrection.

Why had Nippon Telegraph & Telephone abandoned text messaging? It appears that the company did not adopt the strict regulations and short code standards imposed by wireless carriers in many countries around the world. Without this oversight, during 2001 and 2002, DoCoMo systems were overcome by a tidal volume of SMS spam, causing users' screens to freeze and spreading programs that caused the phones to auto-dial emergency numbers. Not good.

DoCoMo announced new antispam countermeasures to cope with an increase in spam sent via Short Mail, DoCoMo's branded SMS. On April 1, 2004 (a somewhat ironic date), the company instituted measures to identify spam sources, which would then be denied access to all DoCoMo services for a specified period of time. If spam continued after the suspension ended, DoCoMo would terminate the spammer's subscription. The company also engaged with McAfee security to install a custom malware scanner on all

in-market phones. This is still standard on all phones in Japan.

By July, DoCoMo had suspended 3,009 lines. Individual users faced difficulty blocking such messages because of their random origins. Soon after this, it seems that DoCoMo gave up. SMS was all but dead. Japan moved to a non-SMS-based Sky e-Mail that had no standard or instant activation trigger for products or mass media. Out of necessity, DoCoMo proceeded to co-opt the QR (quick response) code standard, experimenting with embedding URLs in the code to jump to mobile webpages.

The QR code was initially developed in Japan as an industrial warehousing standard to allow for speed, accuracy, and, most important, the ability to store more data and character types. Now it has become a substitute for SMS discovery that is commonplace in other countries. It was clear that Japan downgraded SMS as a phone feature in 2002 because it lacked the short code standards that are now in place in the United States. Countries such as India are also experiencing a rise in SMS spam. While not as aggressive as in Japan, it is undermining the marketing channel and pushing consumers that can afford the cost to upgrade to closed messaging services run by BlackBerry. Vodafone Essar, a major Indian carrier, has seen its BlackBerry subscriber base surge from twenty thousand to over one million within a year.

Of course, mobile 2-D code readers universally bundled on every handset in a country make for a powerful tool. But even in Japan, contrary to popular assumption, mobile 2-D code adoption is slower than advertised. Seen primarily as a youth channel, it has only 10 percent usage, according to Nobuhiro Ueda at NTT MediaCross.

The reason for this slow adoption is that the primary communication channel is separate from this new activation channel.

NTT is asking consumers to adopt a new "convenience" tool that is outside of their hourly mobile tool set consisting of web, Sky e-mail, and voice.

NTT is only now looking at new channels for premium rate services (PRS) in Japan—presently, there is no channel outside of premium voice services. The only use for SMS in this world is via a service launched in 2009 called Karaden, which allows an SMS with a web link to be sent to mobile handsets. It's a way of moving the consumer to a brand's mobile web. Does this not sound a trifle ironic for a nation that is touted as leading the global charge in mobile?

Myth Busted

There is value in scanning a code. Across the Pacific, many US pundits are sticking to the 2-D code vision and believe that it can gain traction with the North American consumer as a shopping utility.

Similar to NFC tags discussed earlier, the 2-D code is used in three ways:

- **WRITE**: If the *2D code is displayed on the phone screen,* it can be used as a ticket or coupon to show at PoS (point of sale) or PoE (point of entry). The phone acts as a publishing medium.
- **READ**: If the *phone is the reader,* the 2D code can be placed on media or a product to allow for Scan2Web, Scan2coupon services.
- **PEER-TO-PEER**: The phone is the reader and writer allowing for file transfer (business cards, etc.) from one handset to another.

In the first bullet, the phone becomes the product coupon, voucher, loyalty card, gift card, ticket, and so on. We will discuss this implementation in greater detail in the bricks-and-mortar section of this book. Let's look at the phone as a reader.

Newer phones with AF camera and/or video are better readers. They capture a clearer image. This is critical for anyone who dreams of walking down the aisle wanding product info, creating shopping lists, or comparison pricing. These newer phone cameras can scan 2-D codes *and* also scan regular bar codes commonly found on chips and chocolate on the grocery aisle. If the phone can scan regular Universal Product Codes (UPC), the solution can gain critical mass. It will enable users to comparison shop on the go with information on more than twenty million products from more than twenty thousand retailers worldwide.

Alexander Muse, cofounder of the mobile shopping solutions company Big in Japan, located in Dallas, has built his business on Japanese scanning technology. "Combine the local and online pricing results with a dashboard of product data including videos, news, side-by-side product comparisons, and other data, and you get a very rich experience," he says.

With Big in Japan's ShopSavvy smartphone application, users can comparison shop by scanning a product's bar code with a camera phone. ShopSavvy finds the lowest prices online and at nearby bricks-and-mortar retailers and can also provide available coupons.

As for the future, global brands and retailers including Kraft, L'Oréal, Coca-Cola, and Wal-Mart are sitting around the table working on what they called *Extended Packaging,* which involves converting traditional bar codes into data-rich 2-D standards. The

new codes need to house "trusted data" about products, such as expiration dates, age recommendations, and so forth. This may advance business-to-business use of the standard, but many question when consumers will adopt this as a data convenience.

Comparison Shopping:
"The Store Walls Are Porous"

The applicable scenarios for bar code scanning can seem straight out of the 1960s TV cartoon show *The Jetsons*. Walk through your pantry scanning products you need to replace, auto-generate a shopping list, and use this to shop effectively aisle by aisle in the store. Do the same in the store to drive product to the pantry. In theory, it seems a beautiful thing. Alexander admits, "I am not a user of ShopSavvy. It is not for everybody—it depends on your shopping habits."

The messy part is that not all products are indexed. There are lots of "product not found." For ShopSavvy and similar search engines such as TheFind, they need to pull metadata on hundreds of thousands of products in the store. Some stores have dynamic data feeds, but for most it is a challenge to update information easily. Some retailers have open APIs, like Best Buy, but other retailers send flat files. However, in the case of Amazon.com, the only way to access its product data is to extrapolate this off the website.

So-called mobile clearinghouses like Scanbuy and NeoMedia Technologies register the UPC and link (route) the shopper via the QR code to "custom"-branded mobile webpages directly from the physical package. (While QR, created by Toyota subsidiary Denso Wave in 1994, is only one of many 2-D code variations—Aztec Code, Microsoft Tag, and so on—it has become the Kleenex of

codes, its name used generically.) The brand's mobile web address is usually routed through a proxy address, which allows the brand to measure scan-throughs effectively and redirect to a new web address on the fly without changing the in-market QR code.

This scan goes beyond in-store price lookup. By registering the brand UPCs (soup, chocolate, chips) to link to specific content (recipes, discounts, information), the UPC can put the brand back in control of its most important asset: the package. For most brands and retailers, simply pointing the URL to a redirect page for analytics is enough and can be built in-house by the web shop or digital agency.

Most bar code scanning is driven by comparison shopping: scanning the physical aisle to price hunt on the virtual aisle. Electronics, apparel, and sports goods are ideal examples. Scan a code in Best Buy off a Sony Bravia TV and find a better deal online. There is a real fear that portals such as Amazon.com can use their mobile price-check applications to reduce the local store into little more than a showroom. Larger retailers may be able to fight back by stocking exclusive products with unique IDs, making it difficult to compare in-aisle apples to online apples.

But this only forestalls the inevitable. According to the market research firm IDC Retail Insights, upward of 50 percent of "smart" consumers are shopping in competitive aisles. We are in a "new era of price transparency," concedes Wal-Mart CEO Mike Duke. The store walls have become porous, and "everyday low prices" may just not be low enough.

"Most at risk are retailers who sell undifferentiated, easily comparable goods," says Visa's Tom Purves. "Bar code APPs are killing the likes of Best Buy. Mobiles make it so easy to compare prices, make consumers into better negotiators, and drive a lot of

sales to Amazon.com. There are a lot of retailers out there that risk having mobile do to them what the Internet has done to Blockbuster."

But is this a problem or an opportunity? Historically, incumbent industries have battled ineffectively against technology enablers. For example, the music industry embraced digital far too late, alienating the consumer in the process.

The smart shopkeepers will redefine retail. Purves calls this "augmented retail," a new digital layer of experience on top of the physical consumer experience of retail. "Savvy retailers are going start paying at least as much attention to the in-store digital experience of their consumers as they already do to the physical, visual, sonic, olfactory cues that they already obsess over," he predicts. "Augmented retail should let retailers tell deeper stories about their products and their origins and even build services— even billable services—around those products that continue adding value even after the consumer has left the store."

Brands need to embrace comparison, or "informed," shopping. The informed shopper will buy a product for the right reasons. Creating a mobile presence that is simple to access with one click and well optimized for searching will help the shopper select the correct product based on his or her needs and budget, ultimately driving brand affinity.

The local grocery or drugstore, however, is a different proposition. En masse, food and drug products are not purchased in the virtual aisle, so in-store price comparison is not viable for the grocery or drugstore shopper. These consumer packaged goods (CPG) are by and large captive to the retail store. For them the UPC can be a way to enhance and hone the shopping experience.

Proximity Marketing

Brett Bonner, senior director of research and development at Kroger, is taking in-store scanning to the next level. His office is located near the Kroger concept store in Cincinnati, where new ideas are tested. Bonner is in his element using wireless to retool the way that the supermarket chain's customers shop.

"The reality is that people do not task-switch in the store," he asserts. "Maybe in Best Buy a shopper may open his phone to comparison-shop for a thousand-dollar TV set. But not for a one-dollar can of baked beans. There is a fine balance between productivity and price for the shopper."

Bonner understands how to leverage wireless to drive productivity. He was a young pup on the Federal Express technology team where Harry Dalton, vice president of strategic integrated systems, developed the first successful tracking system. "Harry was all about the customer experience. By creating a real-time wireless scanning and tracking system, we created what Harry referred to as a 'custodial control system,'" explains Bonner.

The FedEx corporate tag line was "Information about a packet is more important than the packet itself." Now Bonner is taking this philosophy into the grocery store. He has patented a retail tracking system that allows shoppers to shop more effectively and employees to track their tasks in real time. It also allows Kroger and any store using the system to track the location and/or task on a digital map of the store.

"We made a cheap, rugged, disposable unit that the customer and clerk can use. They can take it home. We put the money in our own network and software," says Bonner. This unit is made for the shopping experience. It optimizes in-store product scanning and

allows for brands to present offers to shoppers in the aisle. Bonner has even patented a reverse-auction function where brands can bid for shopper mind share in-aisle at the point of decision. "We are building our relationship with the shopper and helping them save money. We can put more of the manufacturer's profits back into the shopper's wallet."

But will shoppers embrace a proprietary mobile unit when they already have a convergence mobile device that talks, texts, and surfs the web? "Yes," says Bonner. "CEOs of brands and retailers think they need to use the consumer iPhone because 'they' have an iPhone. All the smartphone shopping APPs that I have downloaded just sit there. And I am trying to use them; I just see no value. They are not optimized for the store."

A definitive store buster is eBay's Buyer's APP, which turns the consumer's phone into a Kroger-like scanner. eBay buyers can use the application to scan products on the shelf and instantly know what these goods are selling for on eBay. If there is margin, they can buy and make a profit. Amazon.com's APP allows for scan-to-compare prices online. These APPs allow for smart arbitrage and are brilliant examples of how mobile scanning connects the commerce dots between the corner store and the e-store.

Without question, code reading is big in Japan and hot in the United States. While codes are a potentially valuable navigational tool, marketers need to recognize that most mobile users will simply open their browsers and perform a keyword search. If the retailer wants to reconnect with this "Trojan" shopper, they need to integrate messaging into the experience to continue the conversation.

One underutilized feature of the QR code is the ability to scan to SMS, text, and even auto-dial a phone number.

Scan me.

Pretty cool. But after shipping thousands of QR stickers to businesses to be used in their store windows, Google's decision to junk its touted QR codes strategy for Google Places signaled that this advertising giant may not believe local shoppers are using its channel to hunt for local business info. It certainly indicated that Google feels that its NFC-enabled Android phones will leapfrog this channel with its new mobile wallet.

Phones enabled for near field communication may sound the death knell for code scanning. By simply embedding NFC-readable tags in proximity media and products, brands and retailers allow customers to TAP to find info, enter promotions, and get rewards. It is a far more frictionless experience for a store, or on the street.

The Japanese mobile mother ship is calling again: Taglet, a Japanese mobile APP, allows NFC phones to associate specific data with any RFID-tagged media or product. Wave the phone over the tag and retrieve information: a Twitter handle, a website URL, a consumer SMS, or e-mail.

- Tap2coupon
- Tap2text
- Tap2web
- Tap2talk
- Tap2tweet
- Tap2locate

Homework: Build Your Own TAG

1. **Buy TAGS**: Think of the TAG as a 64-bit hard drive that you can program and place on any media or product.

 • To buy your TAGS go online and Google "NFC tag supplier."

 • Make sure the TAGS are NFC Forum standard compliant (e.g., MIFARE Ultralights*).

 • Tags can come as stickers, key chains, wristbands—pick your marketing flavor.

2. **Write SERVICE to the TAG**: You need to write a command on the tag that the phone can read and act upon.

 • You can buy a dedicated USB TAG writer, but for this project, just get your hands on an NFC-enabled phone, such as a Samsung Nexus S, that can write to this tag.

 • Download an APP that allows you to write services to the tag (for example, NFC Task Launcher).

 • Services include simple commands such as:

 – TAP2WEB (coupon, APP download, microsite)

 – TAP2EMAIL

 – TAP2TXT (SMS technically; it's not a part of the NFC standard, but will be soon)[†]

 – And then lock the SERVICE or your Coke promotion may be rewritten to a PEPSI promotion in-market.

3. **TAP to read the SERVICE**: The service is now written on the tag and a new NFC-enabled phone can activate this command with a TAP.

* The choice of NFC chip (tag) is critical; MIFARE Ultralights and 1Ks and others have different interactions and features. Ultralights are much faster and can be locked, but they hold only enough data for a URL; they can't even store a full business card. 1Ks store a lot of data, but are slow and cannot be locked. (That leaves them prone to easy hacking by idle thirteen-year-olds.)

† All other NFC services are outside of the basic tags and are defined by the specific NFC application that manages the tags. Proceed with caution if the service needs to be handset agnostic.

Apple Kool-Aid

Bridget Brennan, author of *Why She Buys: The New Strategy for Reaching the World's Most Powerful Consumers*, shows this picture to a bunch of men at a shopper marketing conference in Miami.

Here is a marketing conundrum: statistically, women buy and men market, explains Brennan. Woman rarely feature in the CXO organizational chart. There is a misalignment that, if not balanced, will lead to inefficient retail strategies.

In some ways, mobile is no different. There is often a business misalignment that makes for misguided retail decisions. In mobile, it is not a gender divide but a usage misalignment. Mobile shoppers use their phones in a different way than chief marketing officers use theirs. Our industry uses guesswork a lot. Guesswork will not align the two, but guesswork (unfortunately) often serves as a strategy.

I call this "the CEO's Niece" problem. A CEO goes to her summer house in the country for the weekend and meets up with her teenage niece. The teenager proceeds to show her aunt her new iPhone, finger flipping through Angry Birds and other eye-candy

APPs. On Monday morning, the CEO storms into the office and demands, "What is the company's APP strategy?"

Now, APP development budgeting runs pillar to post. Due to platform fragmentation, custom builds on Apple, Android, Black-Berry, and Windows can cost a hefty penny. Fast-forward through $50,000 in R & D, and the APP is in the APP store. Results are minimal download. As with hundreds of other branded applications, the 5/30 rule applies: after five days, 30 percent of users are returning to the APP. But after thirty days, only 5 percent of users have any recollection that it exists on their phone.

Of course, I am not ignoring the value of hundreds of thousands of applications in the APP store. Apple has done a tremendous job of nurturing its developer community with robust software development kits, or SDKs, making it easy to develop market-ready products in minimal time. This is great for Apple's, Droid's, and BlackBerry's internal marketing and communications strategies. Apple's SDKs are the best marketing spend the company ever made. It's great for Apple's market share, and it's great for a garage developer's vanity—but it's not always an ideal platform for brands to leverage.

Someone should inform mobile consumers that APPs are the place to be. Yet they consistently use mobile web over APP across all information categories:

Top 10 News and Information Categories, United States

Category	App	Mobile Web
Search	6	23
Weather	6	21.5
News	5.1	19.5
Social Networking	6	19
Sports Information	4.2	15.5
Entertainment News	4	15.5
Maps	11	13.5
Photo/Video Sharing Services	3	13
Movie Information	4	12
Stocks/ Financial News	3.5	11

Source: comScore MobiLens, Three-Month Average Ending August 2010

Angry Birds won the Game of the Year Award at the 2011 Mobile World Congress (MWC) in Barcelona, Spain. Rovio, the creator of Angry Birds, is clearly the mobile poster child for a successful APP. Since these exploding and egg-dropping birds debuted, the company has sold over 6.5 million APPs. Angry Birds has an audience, and it has become the gold standard for APP game domination.

At the MWC after party, Rovio chief eagle (founder) Peter Vesterbacka—clad in a swank Angry Birds sweatshirt—discussed APP strategies with me. "It is like producing a hit TV series like *Glee*. Brands do not necessarily go out to try to duplicate its success. My recommendation for a brand or retailer is to work with APPs like they work with television. This will give them audience," Vesterbacka said.

Nielsen's contention is that only five applications are utilized on the consumer's device per month. Maybe we should heed Vesterbacka's advice. After the magic number of five, across all age categories, there is a precipitous drop-off.

How Many Free Downloads from the App Store Have You Made in the Past Thirty Days?

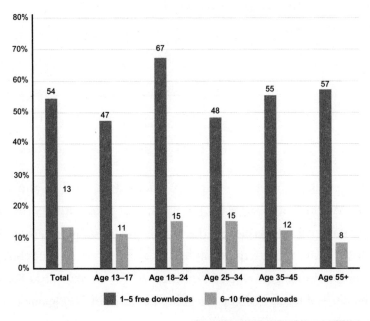

Source: Nielsen Mobile Media Insights survey T2600_1

The Weather Channel, CNN, ESPN, and Angry Birds may have the muscle to command an audience, but it is a limited club. The few successful smartphone applications that capture an audience can follow Bob Pittman's lead from AOL. When Pittman moved from MTV to head up AOL in 1996, he turned the publishing model on its head. He made it all about the carriage fee. Pittman said that AOL, as a major portal, did not need to pay for content, but rather content providers in the portal needed to pay AOL for audience. In the new world of the APP, audience must be king.

. However, why do brands and retailers, who cannot command audience, continue to build miscellaneous APPs? "There is fear, but it is the new reality," says writer Dan Butcher of the newsletter *Mobile Marketer*. "Retailers are becoming aware that consumers are using their phones in the store to make decisions. They're realizing that they need to support that platform." So retailers are mobilizing somewhat irrationally. They are drinking the Apple Kool-Aid. The fear is that if the brand or retailer does not act now to secure a footprint on the APP store, it will be left to play catch-up in the years to come.

The Fifth Slot

The brand can, of course, successfully buy advertising inventory on one of the well-trafficked five APPs (Weather Channel, CNN, ESPN, and so on), but the brand shouldn't have the hubris to think that it will develop a pizza or apparel application that will capture the attention of the consumer long term.

This is the same media paralysis that we have in other vertical markets. For instance, the average American family has 118 cable channels piped into their home but views only 15 of them.

If five is the magic number and these are the key downloads, who plays in the space?

1. Weather APP
2. News/sports/entertainment RSS feed APP
3. Games and m-readers APP
4. Social media (Facebook) and social commerce (eBay*) APP
5. Discretionary utility APP

Discretionary APP? This is your slot. To own this golden mind share on the smartphone screen top, your application needs to be opened each day to stay top-of-mind. Grocery? Pharma? Financial? Maybe, but not necessarily your brand or your content.

As a rule of thumb, if the consumer is not opening your APP out of necessity on a daily basis, stickiness can die fast, and the application becomes downloaded wallpaper. Phonetop roadkill.

Grocery, pharma, or financial channels work because of the daily utility: the shopping list, account data, and so forth. These services have a chance at the fifth slot if they create a simple utility like a replica of the shopping flyer or a mobile equivalent of the refrigerator-bound paper shopping list.

Grocery IQ, for example, is a good "fifth slot" application that allows consumers to create grocery lists, organize them, access coupons, and share lists with others. Shoppers can also take photos of bar codes to add items to their lists and create lists of frequently or previously purchased items.

Another exception includes applications that aggregate con-

* eBay's APPs, with 50M downloads (including all eBay's APPs: eBay, Redlaser, etc. plus across iOS, Android, etc.), fall into the social commerce bucket discussed in a later section.

tent, like ShopStyle, or brands that have hardcore loyalists, like Pizza Hut. But do not confuse novelty with long-term utility in this vertical. Pizza franchisees may lock in incremental millions out of the gate with mobile ordering and incentive discounts, but will the APP continue to command attention on the phonetop? Consumers may drift away when there are a plethora of alternatives and cleaner mobile web options.

The key to winning the battle for the phonetop is to nail discoverability and win top-of-mind with the consumer post download. Your primary activation channels on a phone are messaging and browser. APPs are low on the list of active engagement touch points.

Methods of Interacting

DISCOVERABILITY: Your application is lost on the APP storefront. Gone are the days when an application sold by just showing up in a category. So how do you make the CEO of the household download your shopping APP?

Methods of Interacting

Source: comSource MobiLens, Three-Month Avg. Ending August 2010

There are a number of points of discovery. Waiting for attention in the APP store is the most challenging unless you become one of the chosen few profiled APPs. In most cases, the publisher needs to look to grassroots and viral discovery strategies. Blogs and social recommendation engines are the main crowd sources. In some very rare cases, the APP is virtually loaded on the phone by the wireless carrier over the air (OTA). The Facebook APP is a good example.

APP Distribution Options

- OEM App Stores
- Publisher Distribution
- Third-Party Stores
- PR & Social Web
- Pre-loads

Source: Polar Mobile, Inc.

RETENTION: Let's assume that your APP is *perfect,* and the consumer thinks it is a great fifth utility. Now the real battle: remaining at the top of the consumer's mind. Like e-mail on the desktop, activate SMS opt-in on download and use SMS to update the consumer about deal changes on a weekly or monthly basis.

Apple, Android, and BlackBerry provide alert messaging interfaces for developers. Each phone has a unique identifier consisting of a PIN or serial number. By simply opening the APP and clicking an alert opt-in, the APP developer can send one-way messages to the mobile device. These can be triggered by location or

profile. Although this seems like a seamless substitute for SMS alerts, there are three differences to take into account:

1. There is no relationship with the phone number, only the phone and, more accurately, the APP. If the consumer junks the APP, this umbilical cord is broken.
2. If the retailer decides to move to mobile web presences (like Google did with its YouTube APP), Apple or Android owns the relationship with the shopper, and this cannot be easily ported.
3. APP alerts are *one-way* messages and not designed for the consumer to respond in channel.

In spite of the concerns, I am a believer in the APP utility. When Coca-Cola ran its 2011 Brand APP Challenge, it uncovered a number of valuable services globally. A perfect example of APP utility for brands is the winning submission by content developers Two Bulls. The Two Bulls team built an APP that tracked the location of Coca-Cola's vending machines and allowed the user to hold up his or her phone for an augmented view of the machine. The APP could virtually remodel these key points-of-sale locations across the United States (and the world). It can deliver a video experience, targeted messaging, and storytelling. The solution helps sell more Coke by enhancing the customer experience at a high ROI destination.

Noah Harlan, cofounder of Two Bulls, observes, "The APP may get used only once in a while by a given user—not a Top Five APP by any means—but if it's good, and effective, it gets used when it matters most: at the moment of conversion. For a brand, that's a killer moment."

The key is to build utility coupled with longevity. Can the APP survive the attrition of the phonetop? Will the APP simply become lost? There is no question that an intuitive mobile APP such as the Tiffany engagement ring utility has a niche. Nubile folk can hold their ring on the mobile screen to auto-find their correct ring size. This is very cool! However, would this APP be equally cool in the mobile browser and not as a lingering APP on the phonetop *after* the wedding?

This is a mixed and cautionary tale. Many APPs will succeed in providing targeted utility to technology enthusiasts. Many shoppers are not focused on "What it does" vs. "How it works." If the APP does not make my life easier and is one step removed from my shopping basket, it may not get reopened.

There are ingenious targeted applications for coupons, product research, price comparison, and purchase. While many APPs have a utilitarian and high-ROI role on the phone, ultimately these APP "widgets" are paving the way for richer, centralized mobile web functionality. Maybe the ideal APP for a brand or retailer to consider is just a shortcut logo on the phonetop that opens the mobile website.

Location and Big Brother

In 1890, early advocates of personal privacy were spooked by the invention of the camera and early incarnations of paparazzi. They lobbied for what Michigan Supreme Court Justice Thomas M. Cooley called the inalienable right of the public "to be let alone." Two Boston attorneys, Samuel D. Warren and future Supreme Court justice Louis D. Brandeis, wrote in the *Harvard Law Review*: "Instantaneous photographs and newspaper enterprise have

invaded the sacred precincts of private and domestic life; and numerous mechanical devices threaten to make good the prediction that 'what is whispered in the closet shall be proclaimed from the house-tops.'"*

How prescient.

With location-based services bundled on every smartphone on the market, should we too be spooked? Well, perhaps, as evidenced by the media kerfuffle stirred up by the website Please Rob Me (www.pleaserobme.com) in February 2011. The site used data streams from a location-tracking social network where social folk unwittingly broadcast when they were not at home. With just a bit of coding, the website had created a mobile larceny resource for techno-savvy robbers.

But surely these data can be used for benign, useful pursuits? IBM is promoting its WebSphere Presence Server. Shoppers can be detected as soon as they set foot in a store. Services like this enable real-time mobile coupons and can track shoppers' spending habits and browsing time in various departments. Ideally, this would help the system figure out who might be moved to suddenly buy a discounted item.

However, is there really much difference between "Please help me" and "Please rob me"? Are there just cosmetic differences between the invasive Big Brother from George Orwell's *1984* and a benevolent shopping guide offered by IBM? Brett Bonner at Kroger has a patent on a device linked to a closed-loop wireless in-store network that tracks the behavior of the shopper (and the store clerk), dynamically allowing his team to supply offers or sales

*"The Right to Privacy," Warren and Brandeis, *Harvard Law Review* IV, no. 5 (December 15, 1890).

services contextually. The shopper (and the store clerk) appear as small digital pixels moving up and down the aisle.*

We discussed near field communication and RFID tags earlier. But consider this warning from Ralph Poore of Cryptographic Assurance Services: "Merchandizing folk love it. They have dollar signs in their eyes. But there is a Big Brother side to this technology. Shopkeepers think there is limited range of a few inches because the PoS has a weak RFID antenna. If I increase this strength of the antenna, I can scan and track anything with an RFID tag up to about a hundred meters, depending on environmental conditions.

"I can gun scan the goods on a train speeding down a track and use a more 'persuasive gun' down the line to remove any high-value cargo. I can even track an individual for insidious reasons. If you are a high-value asset, I can use your phone to track and eliminate you. Your phone is a unique signature. Your phone is a trigger," says Poore. Doesn't this seem eerily similar to the 2002 movie *Minority Report*, in which Tom Cruise dodges giant screens projecting personalized commercials based on retinal identification? The Federal Trade Commission (FTC) is on the case.

The FTC was established in 1914 with a mandate to advance consumer protection. In the old world, this was radio, television, wire, satellite, and cable. Traditionally, the FTC was the designated market watchdog of online and, for the past few years, mobile. Back in 2007, I spoke in Washington, DC, on behalf of the Interactive Advertising Bureau at an FTC industry roundtable on mobile. I argued that mobile is a strictly self-regulated industry. The majority of mobile marketing services involve sweepstakes

* http://twitter.com/#!/bbbonner.

and contests, which is traditionally a heavily regulated area. The FTC needs to continue to protect privacy, but the commerce and marketing channels have (apart from a few saber-rattling lawsuits in Florida) shown their commitment to self-regulatory enforcement.

There Will Be Lynchings

It is important to remember that these are early days for the mobile communications industry, and many are waiting for a landmark lynching of a brand overstepping its rights in the pursuit of customer data. On June 4, 2009, Sears settled an FTC challenge on its online privacy policy, or end-user license agreement. Although Sears had presented a detailed agreement to the consumer, checking the Accept box may not be enough. That said, a simple "Turn tracking on or off" check box is most definitely not adequate notice and should be a red flag to anyone tracking a mobile shopper. On June 4, 2009, the Federal Trade Commission announced an administrative settlement signaling that material disclosures regarding privacy made only in a privacy policy or end-user license agreement may not provide adequate notice to consumers. The software application *allegedly* collected personal information without proper disclosure to users. Sears had disclosed the scope of the information tracked by the application, but did so in the middle of a lengthy user license agreement provided to consumers at the end of a multistep registration process. The FTC complaint charged that Sears's failure to adequately disclose the scope of the application's data collection—in light of its representation that the application would track consumers' "online browsing"—was deceptive and in violation of the Federal Trade Commission Act of 1914.

Beyond the FTC scrutiny, the Federal Communications Commission (FCC) is putting the market on notice. The FCC, established in 1934, is charged with regulating communications. In the old world, this was radio, television, wireline, satellite, and cable. The smartphone is blurring the lines between communication and commerce with features such as onboard communication and media distribution. The mobile phone adds the combined utility of the fixed telephone, Internet, computer, credit card, game console, library, radio, and TV, to name only a few. The FCC now sees these as falling under its jurisdiction. Location is its key concern. While location-based advertising is certainly paramount to the FCC's concerns, the agency is also very wary of and/or is looking into:

- how net neutrality may impact mobile
- privacy in general, beyond LBS
- ratings for games and content that are played and/or viewed over mobile devices

With payment coming into the mix, government bodies such as the Federal Financial Institutions Examination Council (FFIEC) will join the FTC and FCC. Convergence brings strange bedfellows.

The FFIEC is a formal interagency body empowered to prescribe uniform principles, standards, and report forms for the federal examination of financial institutions and to make recommendations to promote uniformity in the supervision of financial institutions. It too is an umbrella body that was created when the following government bodies realized that they had commonalities around financial risk management:

- Board of governors of the Federal Reserve System (FRB)
- Federal Deposit Insurance Corporation (FDIC)
- National Credit Union Administration (NCUA)
- Office of the Comptroller of the Currency (OCC)
- Office of Thrift Supervision (OTS)

Ultimately, all these bodies will become forces working together to oversee location, payment, and privacy.

In late 2010, the Obama administration committed to instituting a Privacy Policy Office that would help develop a digital "privacy bill of rights" for US citizens and coordinate privacy issues globally. President Obama stopped precariously short of privacy legislation; however, he recommended a "framework" to protect people from a burgeoning personal-data-gathering industry and fragmented US privacy laws that cover certain types of data. The focus was on "fixed" Internet, but convergence and mobile growth will make this a matter of semantics.

At the same time Obama was announcing his privacy initiative, a lawsuit was filed in federal court in San Jose, California, claiming that Apple's iPhones and iPads were encoded with identifying devices that allow advertising networks to track what applications users download, how frequently they're used, and for how long. Minnesota senator Al Franken, chair of the Senate Judiciary Subcommittee on Privacy, Technology, and the Law, began bounding into the offices of Apple, Google, and Facebook. In April 2011 it was uncovered that iPhones and iPads tracked users' locations and stored the data in an unencrypted file. Does this seem to indicate a busy decade of mobile security and privacy litigation and legislation?

For the mobile consumer, "Big Brother of the mall" is not a warm and fuzzy feeling. There is consumer paranoia about being found, tracked, measured, recorded, and profiled. Most consumers know that if a "cook" searches *cookies,* he will get links to recipes, whereas if an "engineer" searches *cookies,* she will get information on browser tracking. This is called contextual profiling based on the consumer's navigation history: all anonymous. The Interactive Advertising Bureau (IAB) and other industry advocacy groups have demonstrated that anonymous contextual tracking is good for consumers: relevant advertising is better than scattershot advertising.

The key takeaway is that "context" is *not* personal. My friend Randall Rothenberg, CEO of the IAB, argues that while a growing chorus of activists want to tightly control online behavioral marketing, "these proposals are premised on an enormous amount of misinformation—and, in some cases, disinformation sown by antibusiness groups opposed generally to the consumer economy and to consumer choice." As Rothenberg explains, "When you're surfing the Internet, nobody needs to know that you're a *dog.* But providers can learn that you like *dog biscuits,* and serve you content and ads accordingly. Behavioral data is not personal."

"Digital Residue"

Location is one of the most sensitive data analytics. There are a number of emerging location-based data platforms emerging. Foursquare, Betook, and Appcelerator's business is to geo-match the consumer with media allowing for targeted messaging. Wireless carriers have the ability to provide location-based information by measuring the distance of the phone signal from the wireless

towers. It is more accurate in urban environments where there is a greater concentration of towers. GPS on the phone allows for macrotargeting services to help locate and move the consumer to the store, where further message targeting can be facilitated through Wi-Fi, Bluetooth, or ultrasound triangulation. It is one thing to have your anonymous profile tracked in order to help the ad service deliver more relevant impressions and messages, but it is another to have the advertiser tap you on your shoulder and offer you a cup of coffee when you cross a magic location coordinate.

For the consumer, it is the same fear we have of the used-car salesman or the dinner telemarketing call. Even with our eyes wide open and with full opt-in, we are somewhat surprised at being "found" based on where we are. Remember that a text message has an almost 100 percent open rate, which means that a location-triggered message (although fully permission-based) will interrupt my immediate and often unrelated activity and force me to dig for my phone. This may sound like a marketing bonanza, but it will immediately alienate a busy consumer who wants things exclusively on her terms. The shopper doesn't continually want to be concerned about what Sanjaya Krishna, principal and US Digital Services leader at KPMG LLP, descriptively calls our "digital residue." For permission-based messages to work effectively, three things need to happen:

- The consumer must explicitly (not inferred or implicitly) opt in for the service.
- The consumer must expect the communication.
- The reward must outweigh the inconvenience of the interruption.

There is a big difference between sending in your zip code to receive a deal of the week every Friday to redeem in a local store and having an offer sent to you while you're running past the same store rushing to drop off laundry while late to pick up your daughter from soccer practice.

Best Practices

The Mobile Marketing Association has done a good job in advocating best practices in the United States (MMA US Consumer Best Practices, www.mmaglobal.com/bestpractices.pdf). In other jurisdictions, best practices have been further guided by privacy standards.

Combine NFC tags with the mobile browser and you can run some location marketing voodoo. Run a TAP2WEB service on your products. Put an NFC tag and a clear call to action on the product. When the shopper TAPs the product in the store with their NFC-enabled handset, the retailers can immediately identify that the product is within the geo-coordinates of the shop and serve up a *sell-focused webpage*. When the shopper TAPs the product after the purchase (in the street or home), the retailers can identify that the product is *not* in the geo-coordinates of the shop and serve up an *affinity-focused webpage* to drive refill, replenish, and reorder activity.

An NFC tag on its own can be made into a very accurate and verifiable geo-location platform. While GPS location tracking has an accuracy of ten meters, an NFC tag in a specified location (store, concert, station, etc.) will pinpoint the consumer to within a millimeter. If you know that Tag 45 is placed in a store in a product shelf talker, a user opt-in TAP on this shelf talker will allow the

retailer to respond based on the product and the location. This is what Craig Tadlock, the CEO of Wireless Sensor Technologies, calls "Google Analytics for the real world."

Go SO LO

It makes more sense to the consumer to be "located" when he or she actively requests a service. Street-smart mobile users are using GPS to locate themselves in an APP, giving them the added value of navigation and proximally relevant information that they can use *actively*.

Think of permission-based location services as falling into two camps:

- find-me applications (services that send alerts automatically based on proximity to a given location)
- find-myself applications (consumer on-demand request for location information for mapping and social networks services)

"There is a third category," says Asif Khan, founder and president of the Location Based Marketing Association (LBMA). "Location applications can be activated to allow select users to find you—in a mall or entertainment district—and allow for third parties to send relevant offers."

This is part of a growing family of location-based social media networks, or ``lo-so" networks. Many of these lo-so applications try to drive consumer engagement and drive-to-aisle services via GPS location. The goal is to provide incentive to the consumer to cross the retail threshold on the consumer's terms. These services

allow the consumer to check in, tap, scan when he or she arrives at a store, restaurant, club, hotel.

The platforms have shown some success in the food and travel industry, playing on the intersection of mobile and physical ordering or mobile and physical check-ins. Restaurants provide a complimentary dessert or two after consumers have checked in on lo-so from the restaurant using a mobile device. The city of Chicago offered points and badges when tourists and others checked in at designated hot dog vendors.

All this requires location identification. The consumer needs to digitally put up his or her hand and say, "I am here." This hand waving doesn't always need to ride on the GPS rails. For instance, Shopkick doesn't tap GPS, but rather utilizes custom hardware created and installed in partner stores and uses low-frequency signals to communicate. Stores include Best Buy, American Eagle Outfitters, and Macy's. Customers that enter a store with the Shopkick APP open are immediately recognized via the mobile device. (Installing hardware in the store and the need for the shopper to launch the APP are big barriers but a cool example of Khan's shopper-trigger location rewards.) Shopkick alerts the shopper with a message and points toward deals within the location.

Location-based services are simply optimizing what retail shopkeepers have done for centuries: try to find where their target consumers are congregating. Ian Schafer, CEO of Deep Focus, a marketing agency in New York City, explained that in his youth he drove an ice-cream truck. "When I heard that there was a football or baseball game in the area, I would motor off and set up shop. Similarly, the more relevant data we can extract from location-based service, the better we can optimize our digital sales."

retailer to respond based on the product and the location. This is what Craig Tadlock, the CEO of Wireless Sensor Technologies, calls "Google Analytics for the real world."

Go SO LO

It makes more sense to the consumer to be "located" when he or she actively requests a service. Street-smart mobile users are using GPS to locate themselves in an APP, giving them the added value of navigation and proximally relevant information that they can use *actively*.

Think of permission-based location services as falling into two camps:

- find-me applications (services that send alerts automatically based on proximity to a given location)
- find-myself applications (consumer on-demand request for location information for mapping and social networks services)

"There is a third category," says Asif Khan, founder and president of the Location Based Marketing Association (LBMA). "Location applications can be activated to allow select users to find you—in a mall or entertainment district—and allow for third parties to send relevant offers."

This is part of a growing family of location-based social media networks, or ``lo-so" networks. Many of these lo-so applications try to drive consumer engagement and drive-to-aisle services via GPS location. The goal is to provide incentive to the consumer to cross the retail threshold on the consumer's terms. These services

allow the consumer to check in, tap, scan when he or she arrives at a store, restaurant, club, hotel.

The platforms have shown some success in the food and travel industry, playing on the intersection of mobile and physical ordering or mobile and physical check-ins. Restaurants provide a complimentary dessert or two after consumers have checked in on lo-so from the restaurant using a mobile device. The city of Chicago offered points and badges when tourists and others checked in at designated hot dog vendors.

All this requires location identification. The consumer needs to digitally put up his or her hand and say, "I am here." This hand waving doesn't always need to ride on the GPS rails. For instance, Shopkick doesn't tap GPS, but rather utilizes custom hardware created and installed in partner stores and uses low-frequency signals to communicate. Stores include Best Buy, American Eagle Outfitters, and Macy's. Customers that enter a store with the Shopkick APP open are immediately recognized via the mobile device. (Installing hardware in the store and the need for the shopper to launch the APP are big barriers but a cool example of Khan's shopper-trigger location rewards.) Shopkick alerts the shopper with a message and points toward deals within the location.

Location-based services are simply optimizing what retail shopkeepers have done for centuries: try to find where their target consumers are congregating. Ian Schafer, CEO of Deep Focus, a marketing agency in New York City, explained that in his youth he drove an ice-cream truck. "When I heard that there was a football or baseball game in the area, I would motor off and set up shop. Similarly, the more relevant data we can extract from location-based service, the better we can optimize our digital sales."

Gowalla, Foursquare, Loopt, and Shopkick are the buzz in this new media. Google, Facebook, and Yelp are all still toe-in-the-water. (We will know the winner when the term *lo-so* is dropped, and we refer to this new media eponymously as "Gowalling" or "Loopting.")

Cause World is one of the more interesting examples of this mechanism: The application lets the would-be shopper accrue "karma points" by simply walking into a store. By window shopping in any of the member stores, the consumer checks in via mobile and automatically generates points that can be donated to a select charity. No purchase necessary. The customer doesn't have to buy anything in order to gain these karma points.

There seems to be a whole black market of shopping currency in the 2010s. Karma points can be turned into actual dollars to send to charities. Shopkick's "kickbucks" can be redeemed for Facebook credits, songs from iTunes, or immediate cash-back rewards at partner stores. Each community deals in some flavor of incentive greenback. However, the main challenge for these lo-so applications is not the "currency," but rather the mammoth task of growing the network to have critical reach.

Shopkick cofounder Cyriac Roeding describes these services as the "physical world equivalent of an online click." But like online inventory, no self-respecting media buyer will consider your media footprint legit if you do not have all major markets locked. For lo-so to succeed, it has to succeed. While the various social check-ins battle it out for dominance, stay tuned.

Beyond check-in services, can social mobile be our shopping concierge? Applications such as FastMall and TheFind can find the quickest route to stores, tell you the commuting cost, *and* remem-

ber where you parked your car. Deals and coupons can be layered into this experience. Most important, it finds the nearest restroom with a shake of your iPhone.

However, the ultimate extension of all these lo-so services and novelties is lo-so *commerce*. Applications that will succeed (via APP or ultimately mobile web) will provide relevance, drive required reach, and have the ability to combine virtual and physical features to process orders and check-ins. Facebook Places has yet to flex its muscle. These social networks will cross the commerce chasm and tether payment with the account and give incentive for consumer conversion from location to commerce. (More later in chapter 5's section "Social Commerce = License to Print Money." First, let's knock knock again.)

5 MOBILE COMMERCE: KNOCK KNOCK

I met my wife in the Soviet Union, pre-perestroika. She was a military engineer, and at the time I was staying at the apartment of the drummer of a popular Soviet heavy-metal band. (Good story, but for another time.) I spent many months courting her on the snowy streets of Moscow and in the process learned a thing or two about Soviet shopping.

In Russia, in the good old days, you bought what was on the shelf. The question was not "What do I want?" but rather, "What can I get?" If you saw toothpaste for sale, you bought ten, then traded and bartered the rest to fill the pantry and closet. Ironically, failed Soviet economics made for good Marxist citizens, forcing folk to share, loan, and borrow.

When my wife arrived in Tokyo, where I was based as a journalist at that time, she was flummoxed. What should she buy now that she had infinite options and no lines? She was truly amazed at so much selection overflowing onto the *shitamachi* sidewalk.

A psychology professor named Barry Schwartz wrote an interesting book on the subject called *The Paradox of Choice: Why*

More Is Less, in which he contends that the modern consumer has too many choices and too many decisions. This makes the shopper always question the immediate purchase and continue to seek alternative choices. The purchase options are evaluated in terms of *missed opportunities* instead of the opportunity's potential. This, he argues, leads to a lot of unhappy people. (Where is the old Soviet system when you need it?)

Option paralysis perturbs not only the consumer but also the shopkeeper. I think that Professor Schwartz would see the mobile shopper as the ultimate example of why more is less. Let's explore why-more-is-less commerce models and see what is working and why.

Mobile: Where to Start?

The shopper of the 2010s is way ahead of any national retailer's marketing department. She is leveraging her phone as a "mobile mouse" to click, scan, tap, and explore in the mall and in the aisle.

The CMO and the shopper-insight team are looking for some newfangled high-tech way of engaging with this itinerant shopper. The sage truth is that the marketing department is chasing shadows. Instead of focusing on shoppers and how they are utilizing mobile in the store, the team is investigating mobile widgets and APPs that have little to no customer reach or ongoing engagement frequency.

Granted, it's no easy feat for a brand or retailer to cut through the maze of mobile options. Smartphone devices have further complicated and fragmented the mobile ecosystem. While the iPhone, as a dominant player, offers a uniform development platform,

the open Android operating system continues to grow its market share. At the 2011 Mobile World Congress in Barcelona, Android owned the show, positioning itself as the "powered by" brand. Attendees ran from Android partner booth to partner booth, collecting eighty-six Android character pins—many of them landing on eBay following the conference.

Android, Apple, and BlackBerry are vying for the growing digital market. The recent bidding wars for mobile patents from Nortel (Apple) and Motorola (Google) are indicative of industry growing pains. Handset hardware and software dominance has always been elusive. Unlike in the PC world, there is less consumer loyalty. Apple was riding high. Now it is Android. But the cart can be upset within twelve months as handsets are upgraded, broken, and bought. Overnight a marginal player can rise to ranking position. Windows Mobile is the perennial sleeper but still may magically reappear as hardware giant HP's WebOS tablets and phones fail at launch. Designing for these operating environments inflates the cost of developing an application solution. This impacts the individual retailers and brands as well as handset vendors and mobile network operators.

Despite the fragmented ecosystem, interactive agencies with a taste for online web design are excited by the SDKs. The iPhone and its cousin the iPad have heightened the draw to these smartphone platforms. With the entry of Apple into the mobile market, Steve Jobs has taken the function and form of the Mac for a walk.

Apple is a media technology company that decided to go mobile. This in turn forced native mobile device manufacturers such as BlackBerry to push into media. The resulting iPhone is beautiful in form but somewhat of a network data hog, while the

BlackBerry is nimble and secure on the network but less appealing to the media-directed consumer. It seems that according to market statistics, *form* wins over network *function*. AT&T profits have soared on its Apple partnership deal. Network pain, perhaps, but a huge profit gain due to market demand for the media-rich, touch-friendly iPhones.

While media goes mobile (iPhone) and mobile goes media (BlackBerry), and other leviathans duke it out, there is one simple thing that I would suggest considering:

Learn from History

Take a trip back into the 1990s and look at the then emerging trends on the Internet. History tends to repeat itself:

The web browser was becoming standard on the desktop in the mid-nineties. During this period of enormous growth, businesses entering the Internet arena scrambled to find consumer models that worked.

Many companies were lured into thinking that developing applications on the desktop would give them market share and consumer mind share: they did neither. Remember the desktop "widget"?

The desktop became too fragmented and difficult to navigate. As the PC browser matured and the speed of the pipe increased, server-side solutions that functioned inside the browser—in other words, cloud-based applications—became standard fare.

Isolated in the browser, these solutions needed a communication channel to engage and reengage the consumer. They used e-mail as this retention tool.

The APP Is Dead! Long Live the Mobile Browser!

The two factors that helped the PC advance were a mature browser and a mature network. With mobile, we are rewriting history. With the smartphone revolution, APPs are the rage. "I-want-one-too" CEOs are running to their agencies and their information technology department and developing applications that only 5 percent of consumers are returning to after a lonely month on the phonetop.

Steve Jobs talks about APPS and the browsers as two separate platforms. But, not surprisingly, Apple continues to focus much of its energy on APPs. It helps the company market the iPhone. Content helps sell devices and also creates a closed portal where Apple can control the relationship with the consumer and revenue on commerce and advertising opportunities. Apple knows this and is reticent to push in-browser functionality, which would cannibalize its APP-dom.

Since 2009, Google has been downplaying the legitimacy of the APP store. Vic Gundotra, Google senior vice president and developer evangelist, said at a mobile conference in 2009 that the web had won, and mobile phone users would get their information and entertainment from browsers in the future.

When Google moved its YouTube portal from an APP to an m-web experience, it sent a clear signal to the market that the mobile browser was maturing. m.youtube.com is the future of the phone. Not only is the web APP comparable to the native APP, it has a better UI and video quality, and perhaps most important, it cuts through the highly fragmented phone market working on any iPhone or Android mobile browser. The *Financial Times* followed suit by abandoning its mobile APP and launching an m-web portal. Both in the process bypassed Apple.

APPs are moving to the super APP: the mobile browser. It happened on the desktop from widgets to browser. These new browsers are powered by HTML5, which is a fundamental stepping stone from the early versions of the mobile Internet experience and will ultimately be the demise of the APP as a medium. HTML5 supports an "APP-like" experience in the mobile browser. It provides:

- the all-important ability to call out for geo-location data
- access to cache and database, making it possible for mobile developers to store things locally on the device, and making the browser behave more like a downloaded APP
- more in-browser smarts and less time downloading Java-Script code and less over-the-air server authentication on forms
- seamless integration of graphics and video without plug-ins

But outside of YouTube, media integration, and the *Financial Times* news feeds, is HTML5 ready for prime time? David Dorf of Oracle sees a middle road: "While some have estimated HTML5 won't be completely finished until 2022, that's not stopping parts of the spec from being implemented in browsers today," he explains. "However, until more of the spec is mainstream, native applications still provide the better experience for users, at least for the next couple years."

The year 2022 sounds a trifle conservative. HTML5 will allow for key, stable functionality for most APP-like services over the next eighteen months. RIM talks about the BlackBerry "super APP" that delivers a user a seamless, integrated, contextualized, and efficient experience. (Sounds like a browser to me.)

ABI Research cites the emergence of HTML5-enabled web-based applications and services as the catalyst behind the anticipated 40 percent annual growth in mobile marketing through 2015.*

And Speed

Another factor in moving the shopper to the browser is a beefed-up high-speed wireless network. The existing networks were built for voice, with data as a value-add. Future networks need to be built for data. And the future is heavy. Video consumption is poised to explode.

Present networks (as seen in the top corner of your mobile phone) are 3G (for "third generation"). Long-term evolution (LTE) is marketed as fourth generation (4G). Verizon Wireless and AT&T Mobility in the United States and several worldwide carriers are converting their networks to LTE. This demands spectrum (low and high frequencies). Verizon has acquired the necessary spectrum for a hefty $9 billion, and Germany has made the first LTE spectrum investment. China has the spectrum; the question is when it will launch next-generation services. Globally, this clearly signals a commitment to LTE—and a graceful exit of WiMAX as a standard.

LTE will also change the business model for the wireless carriers. Shopper be aware, because unlike all-you-can-eat data packages of yesteryear, the wireless carriers will move to tiered data packages—the "you get what you pay for" models. Interestingly, for carriers like Telekom Deutschland, which is the newly consoli-

*www.abiresearch.com/research/1005125.

dated T-Mobile, fixed line and mobile communications are porting their new mobile business model to fixed line.

However, ultimately LTE is a stepping-stone toward the fourth generation (4G) of radio technologies designed to increase the capacity and speed while diminishing latency on mobile telephone networks.

As David Wood, the coarchitect of the Symbian operating system, explains, "Yesterday's super computer is today's laptop and tomorrow's phone." (Until the Microsoft deal replacing it with Windows's Mobile on Nokia phones, Symbian was used by more than 40 percent of all smartphones globally.) The phone of the 2010s is no longer limited by operating speed or network speed and has enhanced services that allow for a more optimized, targeted user experience.

According to Cisco Systems,* 2010's *mobile* data traffic was three times the size of the entire global Internet in 2000. For an old Internet junky, this is mind-boggling. A big chunk of this growth is attributed to mobile video traffic, which will exceed 50 percent for the first time in 2011. Mobile video traffic was 49.8 percent of total mobile data traffic at the end of 2010 and will account for 52.8 percent of traffic this year.

Data consumption on the 4G network will shake up the existing AT&T-Verizon duopoly. Look for companies like LightSquared to power high-speed wireless networks to Best Buy and 7-Eleven to resell to their customer bases as a Best Buy wireless network or 7-Eleven wireless network: buy a monthly plan with a new computer or on your trip to buy a Super Slushie. This is where retailers

*Cisco® 2011 Visual Networking Index (VNI) Global Mobile Data Traffic Forecast.

and brands need to invest and develop a media strategy over the next few years. "This new mobile web will ultimately be better and bigger than fixed web," says Wood.

The Mobile Storefront: Why More Is Less

"I remember taking the Discovery catalogue online in 1995," reminisced Frank Desiderio, director of technology for Ogilvy & Mather. We were discussing mobile commerce over a beer after an Interactive Advertising Bureau meeting in New York City. "The client literally wanted to take the catalogue and paste the pages online." It took brands a while to understand the value of the browser and the digital click.

Here we were, fifteen-plus years later, and history seemed to be repeating itself. Online storefronts were announcing proudly that they had "gone mobile" by retrofitting the online navigation to the constraints of phone screens with 1,300 plus features or to the dozen or so smartphone screen sizes in mobile circulation. Had they truly gone mobile?

To answer this, I need to jump on my soapbox and question what *mobile* meant from a shopper's perspective. In a world of converging digital formats, multiple screens, and ubiquitous hot spots, when is the traditional online world classified as mobile? Is a Wi-Fi-enabled iPad a mobile device?

To the unsuspecting, the answer is yes. The iPad is unencumbered by a network cable and homebound Wi-Fi transmitters. The lightweight form factor transforms the user into a carefree café crawler and has what in all appearances would be called a mobile experience.

However, upon closer inspection, the iPad and the bevy of tablet copycat devices that have entered the market are nothing close to mobile devices. When the iPad launched, billboard after billboard, from New York to Hong Kong, displayed advertisements of the iPad consumer perched with his slippers kicked up at the end of a comfy couch. All the hand models were finger flipping a novel or family photos on a peaceful afternoon, while a glass of gin and tonic waited offstage to the left.

Hell, the iPad is not just immobile, it is catatonic! The Samsung Galaxy Tab and BlackBerry PlayBook are also two-fisted devices that force the user to prop himself up in a chair in order to tap thoughtfully.

Now, I am well aware that this is a somewhat controversial topic. The Interactive Advertising Bureau's Mobile Advertising Committee meeting was sent into knuckle-popping chaos when the iPad (mobile or not) issue was raised. Is mobility defined by the network, the consumer experience, the device form factor, the business model? But the definition of mobile seems to expand daily, based on the company's marketing goals. *Mobile* is surely a sexy word. Apple has started to use Applespeak to redefine all its "portables" (starting with the clamshell MacBook Air) as "mobile."

Here are the questions to ask when labeling an experience "mobile." These are important criteria, as they will either accelerate or inhibit commerce:

1. FORM FACTOR

Not many of us remember—or would even recognize—the first mobile phone. Trialed in the mid-1940s, used by the Swedish police, and powered by the vehicle, this device could make six phone

calls before it drained the car battery. Over the next five years, Ericsson managed to reduce the battery size to eighty pounds. It took thirty more years to develop a truly "mobile" phone. Motorola's "DynaTAC 8000X" weighed twenty-eight ounces. Nicknamed the "brick," this mobile phone came in a convenient briefcase.

It was only in the early 1990s, when the second-generation (2G) networks moved from analog to digital circuitry, that the industry successfully produced the first truly portable handheld devices. This was possible because companies had made great progress in shrinking the size of the battery, as well as the entire device. Suddenly everything came in smaller packages. Processors and circuits were sized down, paving the way for the first handheld devices that resembled the mobile phones we recognize today.

The handheld device is a miracle in impulse communication technology. Does the new form factor of the Samsung Tab or the iPad allow for the same impulse response? One click removed from a transaction does not work. Taking a tablet out of its protective case or balancing it in your arms is one step removed from an impulse experience. Even the first iPad tablet needed to be cradled by Steve Jobs while he sat in a chair during Apple's Las Vegas launch presentation. Is this really mobile?

Here is the Precambrian analogy:

- After thousands of years of evolution, the consumer is 100 percent mobile.
- The consumer with a mobile device is mobilely challenged but can still function.
- The consumer with an iPad, however, is immobile.

The commerce team has to look at the online experience. Imagine stopping customers at the point of interest online and forcing them to reboot the webpage to get to the point of purchase.

The shopper should be able to surreptitiously glance down in mid-sentence to look at an incoming message or offer. Form factor is key. The mobile phone is synonymous with the term "handheld device." My one-year-old runs around the house with random phone-like objects attached to her ear, saying "'ello"; she never has tried commanding my iPad.

In the new world, there are three mobile flavors:

1. mobile-connected *fixed* devices (televisions)
2. mobile-connected *portable* devices (laptops, tablets)
3. *native* mobile devices (handhelds)

Outside of television screens that are controlled by remote-wielding couch shoppers, let's look at smaller portable and mobile personal screens. A simple way of dividing this small-screen digi-

tal world is to think of two-fisted and one-fisted devices. Native mobile devices are old-school form factor, one-handed handhelds that allow the phone to be an asset to the shopping experience and not act as an inhibitor. While the handheld is still an impediment to an optimal store experience, it is a necessary evil. (Ideally, the shopper needs to be moved into a more upright position to engage with products more fluidly; future phones will allow for better shopper posture.) Portable units, however, totally shut down the store experience for in-aisle browsing and buying.

PORTABLE Does Not Equal MOBILE

2. EXPERIENCE

Is it a *native* mobile-consumer engagement? To be mobile, it cannot just be portable. A mobile device is successful as a discovery, engagement, and commerce tool when it is essentially a mobile mouse. Point your phone at the call to action and click or tap.

When Estée Lauder Companies launched mobile storefronts for its multiple brands, it found that the shopper experience on a small screen changed its design. This led the company to curate its content differently. Jessica Rotnicki-Magaro, vice president of e-commerce for Estée Lauder, explained to me how consumers navigate large-screen devices (PCs, tablets) differently from small-screen phones. "Consumers navigate our online storefronts using the What's New tabs, but on small-screen phones the consumer jumped directly into Top Sellers and Top Recommended, to help them navigate quickly and directly to relevant items," says Rotnicki.

Joe Lalley, vice president of digital products at MTV Networks, a six-year veteran of mobile, says that mobile web is chang-

ing his company's digital strategy. Only *30 percent* of VH1 mobile web surfers ever see the home page. Mobile surfing is about time-sensitive, targeted surfing to micro pages. The traditional top-down navigation does not apply.

The web promised access all the time to everything. The aisle became the "endless aisle" full of products as far as the mouse could click. The mobile web, however, is not about the endless aisle—it is about the targeted aisle. It is about access to a product on a limited shelf, a VIP shelf, just in time, just on sale, just launched . . .

- Physical store is limited aisle.
- Online is limitless aisle.
- Mobile is targeted aisle.

On the handheld, à la carte, deep-menu shopping may not lead to optimal, frictionless checkout. However, quick picks, saving favorites, or creating bundle value packs may help optimal one-click checkout. Likewise, offering monthly consumer refills, replenishment on cyclical products will drive more tonnage into the mobile basket.

The mobile experience can also help close the loop on online storefronts and save abandoned shopping carts from the cyber abyss. According to the 2001 survey data from the mobile transaction network mBlox, 90 percent of consumers prefer multichannel options for interacting with businesses, with SMS topping the list. Mobile messaging can be used to follow up and get the person back to complete the purchase.

With the portable tablet and laptop, the emphasis is not always on closing the deal but rather helping the sales process. From auto-

motive dealers to beauty salons, companies are using the iPad as a personal one-to-one sales aid. The tablet is given to the shopper at the point of decision. (The shopper does not bring it in with him.) In this situation, the form factor and the content work perfectly to drive impulse sales—or a least nudge the consumer in the right direction.

Portable Is About an ENDLESS Experience, but Mobile Is About a TARGETED Experience

So, what is the optimal mobile web experience? When we move from the physical device to the application layer, the same logic should hold true.

"Going mobile" is not the challenge. The challenge is understanding the mobile consumer's behavior: again, experience and physicality. The m-commerce shopping experience needs to be designed for the mobile consumer and the impulse economy. It cannot be designed solely for the mobile screen.

Michael Cooper, vice president of Homedepot.com, explained to me that the industry mantra must move from *shrink* to *rethink* mobile content. "Shrinking the web to the phone is just bad design. The user at home and the user in a mobile environment are completely different. For example, the phone is still a voice device—interactions should drive to the call center. On the fixed web, the focus is to avoid the call center at all costs."

If the goal is to take a legacy media and make it work on a smaller phone browser with limited functionality, then the industry is definitely going mobile. However, taking the tethered online storefront and porting it to a mobile browser may not necessarily make it mobile.

Desiderio agrees. Transferring a refrigerator or lawn mower product page from online to mobile browsers is not simply an ergonomic challenge. Heated discussions about page layout may be the least of your commerce concerns.

What has worked historically? Billions of dollars have been spent globally by consumers off the mobile phone on premium-rate services such as ringtones and sweeps $1 at a time. Now with tethered credit card services, this impulse-purchase behavior can be extended to hard goods purchases.

Successful "Deal of the Day" or "Deal of the Week" SMS alert service can be matched with tethered credit card purchases. You see high conversion rates when the retailer can target interested consumers with unique merchandising opportunities.

Desiderio and I (now on our second beers) are still debating the digital storefront. "The native mobile store must place the consumer experience first," he asserts, "with total regard to the consumer's context and behavior, while also leveraging the unique capabilities of the mobile devices, offering timely (time/location) and targeted (access/offers), with immediate methods of search and purchase—or repurchase!

"Beyond comparison shopping and including elements of social networking for sharing and reassurance, ultimately resulting in more confident purchasing decisions."

REPLY2BUY

TAP2BUY

Now, *that* is mobile.

So if a misguided few are using their online experiences to build their mobile storefronts, and their online stores mirrors their

bricks-and-mortar shops with "virtual shopping baskets" and "virtual checkout aisles," what is a native mobile store model? Is mobile shopping a close relative of the physical store, or is it closer to other commerce models?

Let's take a look at the social dynamics of the phone to further understand native mobile behavior.

Social Commerce = License to Print Money

On New Year's Eve 2011 in Arkansas, 3,000 blackbirds fell out of the sky. Folk immediately began to make connections with similar wildlife deaths around the world: 150 tons of red tilapia in Vietnam, 2 million fish in Chesapeake Bay, 40,000 crabs in Britain. There was a moment of apocalyptic Bible pounding.

However, I am told that an average of 150 mass wildlife die-offs are reported to the US federal government each year. What was different on December 31 was people's ability to use instant social communications to connect dots and spread hype more effectively.

Any piece of information we consume has an instant social overlay provided via a phone camera, a text comment, or a web lookup. Social metadata are connected parenthetically to anything we see or hear. These data have social credibility and authenticity, and linger on a person, place, or product like an indelible bubble. *Reality is augmented,* and it is not returning to normal anytime soon. The phone acts as the social glue tying together information, events, places, and people.

Social by Design

Fact: consumers under fifty years old send more texts than make phone calls. This statistic shocks many who believe that people should talk more.

Be happy: texting and instant messaging are getting us off the phone sooner. We are now becoming more succinct, more effective at arranging get-togethers with friends and family. Perhaps these tools are making us more effective social animals.

Text specifically has struck a needed social chord. I do not want to speak on the phone; I want to use the phone to speak in person more. Today's thirteen- to seventeen-year-old walks around nose to phone (not phone to ear), facilitating more multitasking and interactivity. Ironically, this allows them to be more social. It is simply a new normal.

We live in a world where statistics on attention deficit/hyperactivity disorder (ADHD, or an individual's tendency to extreme multitask, to the point where it is difficult to focus or deliberate on decision making) start at 5 percent and run as high as 30 percent of the general population. ADHD affects the way people process and organize information and manage their impulses. To tackle ADHD, a clinician or teacher would look for useful tools to accommodate learning and decision making. The mobile device may service this role.

ADHD idea hopping finally has a technology match. Texting, Twittering, location-based tagging—all create an augmented reality filter to daily tasks. Whether this is adding value or distracting the shopper, it is clear that the multitasking consumer is the new normal.

This makes one question whether lightly jumping from task

to task is not the *real* normal. Impulsively tapping, nail biting, fidgeting, whistling, doodling, blurting out things, and running from one thing to the next may appear out of sorts in the linear world. However, in the mobile world, the handheld device may have finally offered the needed augmented reality or data overlay to our daily routine, providing a layer that makes us more effective animals. A layer that makes us more effective communicators.

It is also a tool that makes us more effective shoppers. Multitasking behavior is key to effectively emptying the wallet. Bob Parker, vice president at IDC Retail Insights, indicates that the multichannel shopper (using online, mobile, store) spends 20 percent more than the one-channel shopper. But interestingly, the "omnichannel shopper"—the shopper that shops in all these channels congruently—spends an incremental 20 percent, nearly doubling the dollars and tonnage. "This is a hyperconnected consumer," says Parker. "And this is the consumer that the store needs to focus on."

To grow revenue, the shopkeeper needs to understand this modern shopper's social habits on the phone. Does the store need to think of "stores" the same way as other digital media? Mobile is impulse and intermittent two-way communication.

"running l8. luv ya" → dont 4get milk

"meet u @ mall" → B here w/ hannah

Since 2009, for phone users under the age of fifty-four, the messaging function outweighs the calling function significantly. The phone is essentially a messaging device that enables voice. Look at these figures from Nielsen:

Average Number of Monthly Calls vs Text Messages

Source: Nielsen Mobile Media Insights Survey T2600_1

SMS, combined with other communication channels such as MMS, Twitter, Apple iMessenger, APP alerts, and Facebook updates, are all crucial to the shopper. In late August 2011, a number of tweets and SMSs announced the DC earthquake *before* the ground shook in New York and Boston.

Let's conjugate shopping behavior across all the channels:

- TwitterI need to shop.
- SMSIt's a good time to shop.
- Facebook .I bought.
- foursquare.Here's where I bought.
- QuoraWhy did I buy?
- YouTubeWatch me wear.
- LinkedInI'm a professional shopper.

And the message is delivered.

There is a newly minted word, *no-mophobia:* the fear of not having your mobile device at hand. (I like to frame this positively as "yeah-mophilia.") Any buzz or *beep!* gains an instant and visceral reaction. An inbound sound of a text message has an almost 100 percent immediate open rate. For a 2010 survey, the website Retrevo (sort of a cross between an electronics marketplace and *Consumer Reports*) asked consumers how they felt about being interrupted by a text message. Thirty-eight percent of those over twenty-five said they did not mind being interrupted for a message. (But we are not referring to interruption while reading a book.) According to 27 percent, a meal was not off-limits, while 11 percent under twenty-five said that even intimate moments could be interrupted.

When Can You Be Interrupted for an Electronic Message?

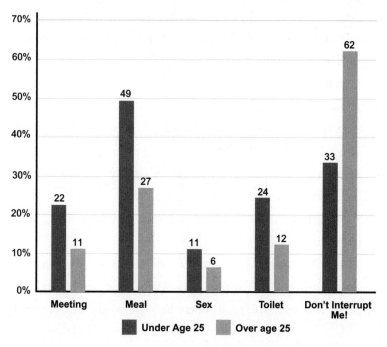

Source: http://www.retrevo.com/content/node/1324

With the under-twenty-year-old millennials eventually overtaking the boomers, there is going to be a whole lot more interrupting happening. Try asking how many of the same sample would interrupt their intimate *mobile* moments for sex? I think few would opt for "mobilus interruptus."

Marshall McLuhan, the grand Pooh-Bah of media in the electronic age, famously wrote, "The medium is the message," in his book *Understanding Media: The Extensions of Man*. I am a believer. We focus too much on the content. Instead we should be focused on the shopper's store, catalogue, and online or mobile behavior. Back in 1964, when McLuhan published *Understanding Media*, he explained that each type of media—television, newspaper, comic strip—is consumed differently. I imagine that he would say the same for the more contemporary PC, tablet, and handheld phone. The *way* in which these media are consumed is more influential than the actual content. To effectively sell shoes or tickets on a mobile device, the retailer needs to understand *how* the goods are consumed on this new medium.

If we accept that this is a new medium and that the shopper is consuming the data differently from other digital mediums, then we possibly need to rethink completely what constitutes commerce on this mobile device. Perhaps we should not start with the premise that m-commerce is to be modeled on the online storefront. Maybe it should be reconceived as an Avon sales force, Amway pyramid selling, Tupperware party, or eBay auctioning engine! Why should it be modeled on a store?

If we look at what m-commerce destinations are performing well, they do not seem to rely on a traditional storefront browsing model. Success stories seem to be where the final commerce

decision is made via phone: just in time on a click-to-buy impulse. Many of these models rely on the social nature of the phone. I call this social commerce: a native mobile-commerce channel built for mobile.

Take a tremendously successful program like Orange Wednesdays, launched in 2004. The success is pure social commerce:

Theaters needed a way to sell movie tickets on the slowest day of the week, Wednesday, so they partnered with Orange (a major European carrier) to offer their customers the chance to receive two-for-one Wednesday cinema tickets. After texting in, the mobile customer receives a two-for-one unique text ticket code that can be redeemed at the box office on Wednesday. The code is entered into the participating cinema's PoS system. A built-in, two-way security system then validates the Orange user and the coupon number before the free ticket is issued.

The results are a testament to the social nature of the program. The incentive program has generated approximately thirty million SMS responses since it began, and Wednesday is now the most popular day of the week to go to the movies outside of the weekend.

How can the brand duplicate this formula? The reason for its success is:

- The offer is based on an immediate need.
- There are no barriers to participation.
- There is a *communication* element that attacts group participation.

The following are five sure ways to succeed in social m-commerce:

1. COLLECTIVE BIDDING

eBay's volume of mobile transactions tripled on a year-by-year basis. The company hit $610 million in mobile transactions in 2009 and nearly $2 billion in 2010, and their public guidance on 2011 is more than $4 billion. This is a bountiful increase over eBay's most aggressive projections. Customers are bidding on twenty-three-foot boats for $19,108 and Steinway grand pianos for $10,000. Not exactly mobile items.

Lorrie Norrington, the former president of eBay Marketplaces, explained that mobile is fundamentally changing the way people shop. eBay buyers and sellers have rapidly embraced mobile commerce, and every year seems to be a mobile commerce tipping point and "shopping," she predicts, "will never be the same again."

Norrington is correct, but the stats and her statement miss one crucial point. The eBay mobile consumer often started as an online, larger-screen consumer. The transaction is a hybrid of online search and tag and mobile bidding.

However, the bidding element is pure mobile. eBay bidding initially leveraged SMS, but the company shifted to an in-browser and in-APP immersive experience. Bidding allows the consumer to connect in data bites, a quick in-and-out mobile browser/APP data hunt. It is social interactivity, and it is the social element that makes it addictive.

The social structure is in place; eBay is simply (and serendipitously) taking advantage of the existing social channel. The shopper finds the item (grand piano, ginger jar, PlayStation console) online in a *thoughtful* environment and then follows and bids in an *impulse* mobile environment.

When Steve Yankovich, vice president of eBay Mobile, designed the mobile bidding process, they actually tested the im-

pulse disruption of checking the product at a stoplight or elevator to see if the heuristics of the site allowed for this m-bid to be executed seamlessly. He calls this the "fifteen-second test."

2. COLLECTIVE BUYING: CROWD SOURCING

Other ideal formulas for mobile can be pilfered from Groupon, the fourth company started by Chicago success story Brad Keywell. Groupon is experiencing startling growth and takes a 30 percent to 50 percent cut of all commerce.

The company is premised on collective buying power, offering users deep discounts on products and services from local businesses. To cash in, you need a minimum number of users to sign up for a deal before the discount is triggered—or in Grouponspeak, tipped.

Like eBay, Groupon is primed to adapt perfectly to mobile and enhance the natural social-commerce element.

A consumer signs up via online or mobile web for deal alerts, specifying where he or she lives and the product category and providing credit information. The company then sends relevant deals via alerts. The consumer replies within a time window to opt in to the "deal." When the required number of shoppers sign up, the deal is triggered, billed, and the community is immediately notified via messaging alerts.

When I met with Keywell, I suggested that mobile is more native to Groupon than to its online antecedent. He smiled. The next week, he announced the acquisition of Mob.ly, a mobile development firm.

Although Groupon has done tremendous service to the industry, it has paved the way for a number of niche crowd-sourcing services. While Facebook, after a short trial, decided to exit the

local-deals business, others will continue to explore the space. Google's Wallet initiative with Google Offers is likely to take over Groupon's market dominance in short order, leaving Groupon's IPO on the rocks.

3. COLLECTIVE RECOMMENDING

Let's push the commerce model further. Let's say that m-commerce can be a game format: take a pavement game with chalk and ball (that you may remember from your distant youth) called four square. It has no equipment, almost no setup, and short rounds of play that you can end at any time. The player with the highest ranking is called the "king," based on handling the ball best.

Foursquare, the retail APP, emulates these key social-game properties. It is a "street game" that is free to download and requires no setup, and the person that gets the highest ranking based on visits becomes a "mayor" and owns a particular restaurant, retail store, or hotel.

Just like the eponymous game, you can start adding friends who also have the APP, or you can start collecting points right away. To become a mayor, you simply click Check In often. The APP will then give you a list of retailers and restaurants in your general area. Click the place where you are, and you start accruing points. Each week, your points are compared to those of all your friends, so you can see just how far away you are from the top or just how close your friends are to usurping your mayor's post. There are even special offers if you manage to become the mayor of your favorite spot. Check the website if you are mayor, because you might have earned yourself a free drink or even a free hotel stay.

Because the APP is a social-network game, it now helps the

retailer drive recommendations across the user's network. Foursquare will alert your game friends that other members have enjoyed it and what their favorite thing to eat is. Besides the many ways of cheating the game by faking location, there are other impediments to growth: mainly its limited reach. As foursquare and foursquare-like solutions grow their user base, retailers will look to monolithic forces such as Facebook to lead the check-in revolution.

4. COLLECTIVE GIFTING

Without question, Facebook is a social mecca—the potential for commerce solutions is significant. Social gifting is one to watch closely. Since 2007, Facebook users were estimated to have spent more than $50 million to send virtual presents: flowers and little puppy graphics to sticker to their profile pages. At an average cost of $1 per gift, Facebook gifts have become an extremely lucrative business. The site has slowly opened up its payment store to third-party developers in order to increase the variety of products sold through the shop.

This gifting commerce is not new and has had a parallel development in the mobile world for years. In the United Kingdom, where buying a mate a pint on his birthday is a time-honored ritual, remote beer gifting has become a great success.

Will Facebook capitalize on mobile commerce? The media giant seems to be betting the farm. Facebook's token system could battle PayPal to become the web's universal currency. In a world where mobile Facebook users check their accounts twice as frequently as online users, it is inevitable that Facebook will expand this payment platform to mobile.

RealGifts on Facebook lets the consumer take virtual gifts into

the real world. RealGifts sells items such as cookies, flowers, and teddy bears in exchange for Facebook credits. You don't need to know someone's address to give him or her a present because Real-Gifts sends that person a notification and requests address details.

But this is just the beginning of Facebook's commerce strategy. JCPenney and 1-800-Flowers.com are working with the social network to allow its customers to shop, share, and buy without having to leave their Facebook account. American Express allows seamless Facebook deal integration to the AmEx member's card. Whether Facebook takes the lead commerce role or partners, alliances between a social network and a retailer or finance player are crucial to grow commerce opportunities.

5. COLLECTIVE COMMUNICATIONS

Facebook is a poster child for the social movement. The company has become an identity clearinghouse for its members. Executives at Facebook explain that their company is not simply a space to *share content* but an instrument that uses this content as building blocks for the member's identity. The network's value is its ability to *connect identity* with brands, friends, and family.

Facebook Like and Send have become social "glue gun" terms connecting and driving affinity among brands, retailers, and the largest identity network in the world. Using Facebook log-in on m-commerce sites can reduce friction and mitigate drop-off. A single-click process is the key to impulse mobile engagements. One simple and effective business idea is to use Facebook on the commerce confirmation page to allow for viral postpurchase sharing. Helping the user navigate a growing, fragmented data cloud, Facebook Connect is a permission profile passport that consumers can use to share their profiles and move their "taste information" on

demand between multiple websites. This allows these websites to deliver relevant, customized content to the user.

The social network has become the essential mobile content bundle for any phone in market. "Can I use this for Facebook?" is a phrase many phone buyers are asking. The new Facebook phone (optimized for social networking) and the Facebook mobile APIs bring these two worlds of mobile and social inevitably closer.

But as the Facebook leviathan is quietly waiting to fully leverage its power in the mobile world, there are opportunities for other social tools to differentiate and drive value. Facebook is all too aware that Google+, Google's new social media project, is poised to link social to its mobile wallet.

There are holes in Facebook's seemingly invincible position. Let's look at a sleeper solution that has drawn grassroots loyalty from hardcore Facebook folk looking for a more insider social tool. Similar to the grassroots popularity of SMS, communication tools can be born while the industry is busy doing other things. BlackBerry Messenger (BBM) is surprisingly popular with teenagers to network parties, share images, and set tasks and challenges (that is, take a picture of X or get a dance with Y). We have seen the power of the BBM network for sanctioned and nonsanctioned social behavior globally.

Facebook has single-handedly changed our definition of a friend. In Facebook land, we may have hundreds or thousands of friends. In BBM world, we have a smaller circle of friends. BBM has struck a chord with mobile users that want to reinvent intimate, rich communication. Unleash this power to brands to run targeted shopping challenges to retail loyalists, and we immediately have a new social-commerce channel with more peer credibility.

For any social-commerce strategy to succeed, the social element

needs to become more mobile. Inevitably, the discussion needs to be mo-so (*mobile* opt-in attached to *social* check-in) or so-mo (Facebook *social* promotions that use *mobile* to engage the consumer via a phone number opt-in to send a coupon or extensible value that can be redeemed in the real world).

The social aspect is an indispensable pillar of m-commerce. When brands and retailers want to invest in mobile, they now need to invest in understanding the existing social patterns and social-networking business models that have been adopted on the phone.

6 CRACKING BRICKS AND MORTAR

In 2005 Procter & Gamble came out with the revelation that brands have three to seven seconds to win the consumer in the aisle. P&G called this the First Moment of Truth, or, in retail-speak, FMOT. (I have no idea why certain initial and acronyms are adopted en masse, but there is an "Initialism and Acronym Hell" appendix at the back of this book.)

The Cincinnati-based company proceeded to assign FMOT directors to develop FMOT marketing strategies to win over the consumer in this shopping inflection. They created products that popped off the shelf, flashy in-aisle displays, and elaborate store TV networks. The director of FMOT and her team work to develop the type of store displays that can win over customers in the aisle. It's an all-out war to win mind share on the shelf and convince shoppers to buy Tide, Crest, and Pampers.

P&G went on to move large chunks of its traditional media budgets to in-store digital and point-of-purchase displays. The consumer-packaged-goods giant understood that its media buying agency would naturally gravitate toward costly TV spots, so it

began to tie ad agency compensation to increased sales and key performance indicators (KPIs)

This retail intervention is called shopper marketing: tactics to influence in-store consumer behavior by way of in-store displays, sales, packaging, promotion, research, and marketing. Karen Stermitz, shopper marketing and mobile evangelist at Hewlett-Packard, refers to the five-by-five shopping universe. (That's five feet of aisle space by five seconds of shopper attention.) "The brand needs to work to develop a consistent, clean message across all the media touch points," she emphasizes. The messaging, icons, and imagery need to remain consistent and be reinforced down to that five-foot-by-five-foot space of decision making in the store.

This rallying cry is somewhere between urgent and desperate for retailers and brands that feel they are not effectively engaging and influencing the shopper at the point of decision. What is influencing the shopper across the retail touch points? What is making the consumer select my product? They want to know.

The store, some lament, is becoming an expensive catalogue. Statistics compiled by ARC Worldwide reflect this trend. Only 25 percent to 30 percent of shoppers find the physical store to be a stimulating environment that introduces new products. The Internet is accounting for the bulk of shopper engagement on new products. Does this leave bricks and mortar with nothing but bricks and mortar? Retail analysts suggest reinventing the store as a place to taste, touch, and feel the product. These are features that online cannot provide. Complimentary yoga classes at Lululemon Athletica clothing stores, Williams-Sonoma cooking classes, Home Depot workshops on various skills, and Toys "R" Us family entertainment are good examples. Use the store to connect emotionally with your customers.

ZMOT: Zero Moment of Truth

On March 29, 2010, Jenny Liu, senior product manager at Google, posted on Google's *CPG Blog,* "While this first moment of truth is still important, the rise of full Internet adoption and increased search engine use often leads to many brand interactions taking place between a consumer and a brand before that consumer ever sees a product on a shelf. This phenomena is what we are calling the 'Zero Moment of Truth,' or ZMOT."

Ken Coogan, who runs brand strategy retreats with dozens of major consumer brands across the United States, agrees that manufacturers are wrong in calling the store the "first moment of truth." The reality, he says, is that "we all enter stores with pre-conceived ideas about brands, and the store is the *final,* not *first* moment." The trick is to reengage the shopper in the aisle, remind her of the brand, and close the sale.

Google's ZMOT is simply the consumer starting point in the internet cloud for a path to purchase. Good marketers will use every opportunity to intercept the shopper along this path. Shopper marketing is nothing more than ABC sales principles: *"Always Be Closing."*

Before we cancel our store leases and move into the cloud, we need to understand the hybrid value of the physical and virtual store and the symbiotic roles they play. We need to acknowledge how much entertainment and social value the store provides. The physicality and proximity of the product will always play a key role in the shopping experience. Shopper marketing will continue to sway our decisions on product selection.

Robert Woodruff, Coca-Cola's chief visionary from 1923 to 1954, told his team that their product needed to be within an "arm's reach of desire." Doug Busk, head of Coke's mobile strat-

egy in 2011, puts Woodruff's vision in a contemporary context. "There are between 1.6 billion servings of Coca-Cola and 5 billion devices," he says. "Just about every hand around the globe has a mobile phone. We'd like a Coke in the other hand of everybody with a mobile phone."

Shopper behavior is a niche science. For years, the only measurable shopping metrics were your sales reports. Coca-Cola, Diageo, and Unilever have worked with POPAI (the Global Association for Marketing at Retail) and its Marketing at Retail Initiative (MARI). MARI's goal is to physically conduct studies in stores to establish more practical metrics that can be used to change store layouts and interactivity. The deep-dive studies that POPAI continues to run in stores across the country use:

- **CLIPCAM**: shopper-worn cameras fitted to their glasses
- **DIGITRACK**: camera technology that records, measures, and analyzes each shopper's behavior characteristics: speed, location, and behavior together with the time spent looking at each display

This is giving a true picture of shopper behavior. The MARI study offers the first real opportunity to see the store as a medium and a media. These scientific metrics are validating retail lore that of all the consumers that pass by, only 6 percent are converted to a sale:

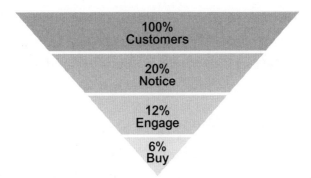

The study measured:

- the total number of shoppers in the store
- hot and cold shopping zones
- shopper "dwell time" at a display or product

This should help retailers and brands answer where the problems are in the store and what can be done to drive more sales and influence the decision-making process of the shopper.

Retail pundit Dr. Hugh Phillips attributes much of shopper behavior to the focus on product selection. The shopper's in-store attention is driven by her immediate interests. Let's say that I need to buy a candy bar. If my usual brand of choice is a Mars chocolate bar, then I will look for a Mars bar. But in order to focus on selecting that particular candy bar, I'm actually *de*selecting what is not relevant to the task in hand, such as magazines and other brands of candy. The brand has to invest in engaging with the shopper at this point of myopic, targeted selection and sell him on its brand.

(This idea is not novel, incidentally. The French writer Jean-Paul Sartre—not a hard-core shopper—wrote about the human experience of negation. In his 1943 book *Being and Nothingness,* he gave an example similar to the candy bar shopper. A person enters

a café to meet a friend, "Pierre." In order to find Pierre, he *deselects* all people who are *not* Pierre. We do the same thing when we're shopping and are looking for some*thing* as opposed to some*one*.)

Shopkeepers and Shoppers

If, according to Winston Churchill, England is a nation of shopkeepers, then America is surely a nation of shoppers. It is coded into our DNA. If you want to win the battle in the aisle, you need to stop chasing the *consumer* and focus on the *shopper*. The two approaches are different. To the brand, the consumer is the general shopping masses, while the shopper is the actual Joe Shopper buying products in the store. Instead of spending an endless sum on mass media, the brand can invest a more targeted amount on the shopper in the store.

If the consumer = potentiality, and the shopper = actuality in the store, where are you spending your media dollars?

Lisa Klauser, a fifteen-year veteran at Unilever, is now the brand bearer and vice president of customer solutions. She is mapping the process that takes place from the moment the shopper first considers purchasing an item all the way through the selection of that item.

"Shopper marketing is the ability to mine insights and then translate those insights into actionable programs or solutions with our retail customers that are going to drive our business," says Klauser. "The proliferation of mobile devices and use among consumers to share information—Facebook, Twitter—and savings—downloading coupons—provides another consumer touch point. We're able to connect with consumers in a way that is relevant to

them, promoting our brands and products in real time in-store and everywhere else they carry their mobile device."

The brand needs to counter by working hard to understand shoppers better and their in-store behaviors. The store needs to accept that the shopper does not fit into the historic paradigm. If the retailer places the shopper at the center of the world and sees the store through her eyes, then the mall stores fall into the following matrix:

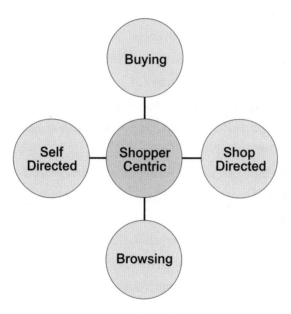

These shopping clusters can be mapped on a chart based on their shopping modality. Is the price-directed shopper buying or browsing? Is the shopper open to being store directed, or does she want to be left alone to self-direct? How can you surprise and delight rather than interrupt and annoy? The retailer needs to look through this lens to develop an engagement strategy and, more important, a compelling value proposition for the customer.

We mentioned Paco Underhill's store research earlier. Underhill spent many years observing the shopper in the aisle. Based on these data, he wrote the definitive bricks-and-mortar book, *Why We Buy: The Science of Shopping.** After two decades, what did Underhill learn?

1. Shoppers turn right when they enter a store. He called this the invariant right and attributed it to the fact that most folk are right-handed. Insight: place your sexy merchandise on the right side of the entrance.
2. People don't read more than four words in the shop window. (And that was *before* mobile.)
3. Shoppers accelerate when passing by a bank.
4. Mirrors make shoppers feel self-conscious and as if they're being "watched."
5. Put a chair out in a clothing store: men sit and women shop longer.

Underhill's biggest insight, though, was that open spaces, bathrooms, and seating are all as critical to sales as pricing and visual merchandizing. Thanks to work such as Underhill's, the science of shopper marketing has exploded. There is a school of thought that sees the entire "store as media." Ironically, the store is learning from that last decade of online digital shopping and taking this off-line. The retailer is infusing bricks and mortar with the interactive goals that the consumer and brand discovered online.

Retailers and brands alike are spending more money on in-store marketing. These budgets go toward in-store promotions and

* www.amazon.com/dp/0684849143.

media that "interrupt" the shopping experience and help shoppers select their products. As the store experiments with expensive interactive screens tethered to the shopping carts and in-aisle kiosks, how can these screens connect more effectively with the consumer's personal screens?

Andrew Harrison, CEO of Best Buy Europe, explains that there are multiple media platforms in the store, and they all have shopping screens. "Screens are portable, handheld. They live in the store, but they also live in the shopper's kitchen, bedroom—even their toilet. This screen is the new battleground for media this decade." The retailer had better be consistent, fluid, and frictionless across these screens. (For example, how can kiosk screens in the store allow shoppers to seamlessly transfer product information to their phone, enable a wish list to be accessible on their tablet, and trigger mobile coupons that bring them back into the store and move them fluidly through PoS?)

If Underhill's big insight was that *open spaces* were critical to driving sales, then Harrison's big insight is that *private spaces* (or private screens) are critical for sales. For retailers to succeed this season, they need to understand their shoppers' screens. Creating a consistent experience across these screens is key to unlocking revenue and essential for any long-term strategy.

So where do shopper marketing and mobile intersect? When is it a value-add to the shopping experience, and when is it a valueless gimmick?

Inattention Blindness and Other Maladies

The shopper is mobile. Ironically, the mobile phone is an *impediment* to this mobility. The more effective the mobile phone is, the

more it adversely affects our mobility. If you actually consider the mobility of the consumer in the store and then slap a mobile phone on his ear or between her thumbs, it greatly reduces not only mobility but also cognitive and motor skills.

Illustratively: a 2006 University of Utah research study showed that if a person slaps on a handheld or hands-free phone while driving, their performance behind the wheel is substantially worse than an impaired person with a blood alcohol content of 0.08 percent—the point at which a person is considered legally intoxicated in the United States.

Of course, the cell phone is often singled out as a scapegoat for all possible driver distractions. According to a 2010 study by the Highway Loss Data Institute, banning mobile phones in cars did not reduce fender benders. Equally culpable was probably applying lipstick, eating French fries, or digging for toll change while driving.

But mobility is perilous. More than 1,000 multitasking pedestrians visited US emergency rooms in 2008 because they walked right into a pole or fell off the curb while texting or talking on a mobile device. That is up from 500 in 2007, and approximately 250 in 2006, according an Ohio State University study.

In 2009 Professor Ira Hyman from Western Washington University dressed a student as a clown and asked him to unicycle around a central square on campus. Hyman and his team observed and interviewed bystanders and published a study in the journal *Applied Cognitive Psychology*. Only 25 percent of the mobile phone users said they'd noticed the clown, compared to 71 percent of people in pairs, 61 percent of people who were listening to a music player, and 51 percent of people on their own. The term coined for such a preoccupation is "inattention blindness,"

meaning that a person can be looking at an object but fail to process what it is.

It has become a national security issue. Lawmakers in Arkansas and New York have proposed restrictions on the use of pedestrian phones. Arkansas state senator Jimmy Jeffress lobbied to ban pedestrians from wearing headphones in both ears while on the street or sidewalk, and New York state senator Carl Kruger has similarly proposed banning pedestrian use of electronic devices while in crosswalks of cities with populations of one million or more.

The phone shuts down hand usage and reduces vision, thought processes, hearing, feeling—and, ultimately, the ability to shop. The challenge for the retailer and brand is to find that delicate balance between engagement on the mobile and engagement in the aisle.

One can question whether augmented reality (AR), which allows the consumer to hold up the phone to a shopping aisle and see overlaid information, is an asset to the shopping experience or distances the consumer from the physicality of product selection.

While it sounds intriguing for the shopper to be able to hold up her phone to a street or a shopping aisle and see metadata such as restaurant or product recommendations and details, the service is asking mobile shoppers to become immobile. They need to find and open an application that is not readily used during the course of the day and look for information that may be more readily accessed via mobile web.

(Even augmented reality games like Dentsu's iButterfly coupon game, which was wildly successful in Japan, are one-off campaigns. The game allowed shoppers of certain stores to collect vir-

tual butterflies and the attached discount coupons. Dentsu called it an experiment, and iButterfly now lives on the web as a case study. Mobile gamers swatting fighter planes or demon mosquitoes flying around the viewfinder will tire soon once the gimmick fades.)

Mobile solutions, such as augmented reality, can be useful to the retailer or brand, but is the technology leading the strategy, or does it follow the business need?

If the mobile solution is poorly conceived, it can make the mobile shopper myopic and distract from the goal of closing a sale. Let's look at what works and what doesn't.

Retail: "Offline Interactive"

A modern-day grocer or pharmacy is not a friendly zone for the brand. Gone are the halcyon days, when brands worked hand in hand with local store owners to sell stuff. Now many retail chains compete on the shelf with competitive generic brands.

One leading grocery chain executive told me that "presently the brand makes ten cents, and I make one penny. By the time I finish with the manufacturer, they will have one penny, and I will have ten cents. This is the correct split." In Charles Fishman's book *The Wal-Mart Effect: How the World's Most Powerful Company Really Works—and How It's Transforming the American Economy*, he writes about the store's ability to turn the clock back on inflation. "Wal-Mart has outgrown the rules," says Fisher. However, this is mainly on the backs of brands that have had to dramatically cut margins to service the megachain.

The brand's product and the retail aisle have been locked in an adversarial relationship for quite some time. The product sits

on the shelf, presumptuously hoping for the consumer to recall its catchy jingle, celebrity endorser, or signature packaging, with little to no help from the retailer.

As we have discussed, gone are the days when the brand focused on driving the consumer into the store. Now the brand sees the *store* as media to engage and sell the shopper. But the challenge is that media, packaging, display, shelf plan, and sales promotion are still developed independently of one another. The shopper, however, sees this all as one. The brand needs to do the same.

Traditional store promotions are a mess to manage from start to finish. Store managers complain that promotions often cannibalize the bottom line, to say nothing of the hidden costs of execution. End-of-aisle (end-cap) promotion logistics are also unwieldy. Promotions are displayed too soon or even at the wrong store.

Siloed in-store spending is not working, with $30 billion spent on cardboard and plastic to create end-of-aisle CPG displays. The niche vertical is called "contact packaging," and it consists of approximately two thousand small companies across the United States. Their sole mission is making your product "pop" in the store and drive more sales. For example, they will rewrap Coke bottles with promotional images of *Avatar*, as well as create cardboard castles and creative product stacks. In short, these packaging companies are the *bling* of retail.

A troupe of detailers then visits the stores to check and sign off on the final production. Retail end-of-aisle display detailers are responsible for going to the store and eyeballing the final display, taking a photo for the brands' records. They conduct either random or nonrandom checks of in-store displays to make sure

that the products are showcased as planned. They may count inventory of the displays to see if they need replenishing.

Money spent on end-cap displays in retail stores is set to grow to $50 billion over the next few years because manufacturers are behind the eight ball. This is especially true of the grocery, pharma, games, electronics, and hardware verticals.

Is it effective? Not really.

- In an average-sized supermarket, there is a mess of 4,600 display items.
- Less than 20 percent of shoppers even glance at a display.
- Only around 6 percent take any action.

How can these brands engage the in-store shopper and drive sales more effectively *without* the prohibitive expenses of cardboard, plastic, and detailing? The answer is evident if we revisit the manufacturer's core goals:

- Connect with key consumers (those who spend money with you but have more discretionary cash in their wallets).
- Create personalized, targeted, just-in-time messaging.
- Drive incremental revenue.
- Opt in and retain these key consumers.

Simple. The manufacturer *can* do this without mobile. It just costs a whole pile of money. The brand has limited in-store metrics to identify the most effective spend. Mobile is a cost-effective, measurable one-to-one channel. It allows in-store media to be more effectively leveraged and interconnected.

The Wal-Mart digital display network has deployed end-cap

screens in the chain's grocery and health and wellness departments. The network also integrates mobile call to action across channels via SMS, offering recipes and other added values. In one recent campaign, Wal-Mart shopper participation more than tripled when combining SMS and a strong call-to-action on the digital screen. "There can be powerful synergies between the large in-store screen and the small mobile screen," says Tom Opdycke, CEO of DS-IQ, which provides shopper-marketing technology to Wal-Mart.

The Shoe Flip: TXT, Scan, and Tap

To be effective, mobile cannot lead the charge—it needs to follow, watch, and learn. The mobile-solution providers have to speak shopper-marketing speak. I am not referring to the semantics, but really understanding brands' marketing goals. Currently we have brands and mobile-solution providers using the same terms but meaning different things. It reminds me of the Irish writer George Bernard Shaw's jab at England and the United States: "two countries divided by a common language."

The retail shoe brand Steve Madden has a mobile guy who "speaks retail." The company had just launched a mobile storefront, and Andrew Koven, who heads up its digital commerce division, was now faced with the inevitable mobile dilemma: discoverability. "Build it, and they will come" would seem to be a good strategy for his demographic, since Steve Madden shoppers overindex for mobile consumption.

But how does Madden proactively drive consumer acquisition, retention, and frequency to this mobile storefront? More important, how does Madden use mobile to cross-market across all its

media touch points: physical store, online, direct-response channel, and now mobile?

I met the Steve Madden commerce team at a bustling Steve Madden store in New York at Thirty-fourth Street and Fifth Avenue. We spent some time watching the shoppers enter the store and move down the display looking for the perfect shoe. They seemed regimented and focused on the task at hand, moving up and down the store, eyeballing the selections. Andrew Koven's goal was to find out how to use mobile to activate the physical shop to drive targeted mobile opt-in, to identify a mobile CRM channel that could drive retention at the store level as well as an online acquisition. So where is the ideal point of mobile engagement in the shoe store?

We identified one consistent behavior: "When the shopper is interested in a particular shoe," he noted, "she immediately flips it over to view the bottom tag to see product details." We took to calling this the "shoe flip." Whether the shoppers bought the shoe or not, the shoe flip was a clear indication that they were interested. The shoe flip was the ideal point of engagement. We looked at a shoe tag at the bottom of each shoe:

Shoe Name: Hannah
Color: Blue
Size: 7.5
Price: $39.00

Suddenly the proverbial lightbulb blinked on above Koven's head.

"What if we print a mobile call to action on this tag to text the shoe name to the Madden text short code and create a person-

alized mobile wish list?" he suggested. "We can text them back with shoe updates. Perhaps dynamically populate their mobile web favorites." Now for the clincher: "We can even let one shopper win their wish list."

"I like it," said Lisa Safdieh, the senior merchandising manager. "We now can drive the shopper back to the store based on this wish list; extend the aisle to the street. What I really like is that we are not changing store operation behavior, just one generic line on the shoe tag. Nice."

Steve Madden is one retailer that has committed to the mobile channel, launching an m-commerce storefront, social-media store integration, and a strong SMS and MMS activation and retention channel to drive cross-channel activation.

Koven explained: "At Steve Madden, we do not know what ultimately will work in mobile, but we need to roll the dice if we are committed to finding the right mobile model. Some brands are sitting at the table, and some are rolling the dice." He smiled. "Come back to me in a few years when you decide to write the *History of the Mobile Shopper*. By that stage, we may know what definitely works."

Another footwear maker, New Balance, is also approaching mobile commerce innovatively. Instead of letting its shoes sit passively in the store, the company similarly tagged the product with a call-to-action keyword. But New Balance's goal was different than Steve Madden's. By text messaging the shoe, the shopper instantly opened up a two-way relationship with a New Balance sales expert:

> **Runners with normal to high arches appreciate the comfort & support of Ortholite foam and Stability Web. Try them on and reply "Next."**

Not only is this a more effective in-store sales process for New Balance, it also allows the brand to engage the consumer in a poststore mobile survey, opening a valuable dialogue. Based on whether or not the person bought the product, New Balance can position itself as the next shoe purchase.

> **Why did you purchase New Balance?**
> **(Multiple choice: Fit/Comfort, Style, Price, Other.)**

The New Balance and Steve Madden simple in-store activation examples can be also triggered by a 2-D code on a product and an NFC tag on a product. The immediate goal of the seller is to make the trigger simple and intuitive. Whether you txt, scan, or tap, the ultimate goal and consistent goal regardless of which mobile mouse you choose is to move the shopper in a two-way long-term relationship.

Brands are creating a new executive role in their organizations that is responsible for reaching the consumer. This executive's sole

job is to circumvent the retailer and start a direct relationship with the shopper.

So how does the retail manager redesign the store to win mobile mind share and start to build this relationship?

Put an *M* in Front!

Take all the existing communications hubs in the store and see what can be done to facilitate heightened functionality and inter-activity via the shopper's phone.

- **m**-rebate
- **m**-FSI (free-standing insert)
- **m**-coupon
- **m**-receipt
- **m**-end cap (end-of-aisle display)
- **m**-product fact tag
- **m**-survey
- **m**-kiosk
- **m**-gift card
- **m**-product tag

We have already spent time at the Steve Madden store turning product tags into m-tags with a simple one-line mobile call to action. Here are some other examples:

M-GIFT CARD: InComm, one of the major gift card distributors in the United States, suggests that the plastic gift card "malls" located in high traffic areas at most major retailers nationally are, per square inch, the highest-margin real estate in the store. Shop-

pers spin the display, and eyeball and fondle the cards. Whether they ultimately buy one or not, it is a perfect opportunity for the card vendor to develop a relationship.

For example, by simply tagging each card with a mobile call to action, the person who is looking, exploring, reading the card can be activated. For example, XBLOX live can use txt, scan, or new contactless tags to allow interested shoppers to opt-in to receive offers, preorder games, and find out about virtual collector cards. The brand can segment the banner retailer (7-Eleven, for example) and drive targeted promotions back to the partner store.

The plastic card is fast becoming virtual currency. John Anderson, who heads up GroupCard, a wholly owned subsidiary of InComm, is transforming the gift card into a personalized currency that can be traded and moved across social networks such as Facebook. Making plastic interactive allows for value-added services such as card balance and location-based top-up locations information. More important, it allows the retailer to promote related targeted deals back to the cardholder in a timely way.

InComm will provide mobile balance query and top-up location finder functionality with its new prepaid Vanilla Visa Card. Simply text message the card number and receive instant information to your phone.

Over the next few years, shopper loyalty including points, single-use couponing, and promotion will be combined with the prepaid card swipe at retail point of sale and will be crucial to the growth of this multibillion-dollar industry.

M-FSI: As flyers and direct mail lose their luster and marketing managers look to eliminate these untargeted drops on the consumer's doorstep, mobile may offer a way to reinvent the old channel.

Mobile can heighten the value of the traditional paper and provide a more targeted relationship with the would-be shopper.

Take the four-page grocery flyer and reduce it to one page. Then make it "interactive" or "offline interactive" by allowing the consumer to use his phone (mobile mouse) to take a deep dive into categories. By simply putting keywords and scannable codes on the paper flyer under each category (meat, dairy, health, and so forth), you have a "poor-man's iPad."

Publish one door-buster deal, and the phone can be used on demand to text or scan for deeper layers of offers via the mobile browser. Offers now are self-selected and (if SMS is used) open a one-to-one CRM connection with the retail store.

This off-line interactive channel allows the retailer to instantly alert the consumer to "distressed inventory." Because of lead time required, printed paper could never do this. So let's say that a manager just received a shipment of twenty cases of ripe tomatoes. She can proactively alert the mobile VIP shoppers about a deal for 80 percent off tomatoes. Crowd source and lure shoppers into the store.

Ask your shoppers to txt, scan, or tap for "GREEN" flyers in their shopping area. Allow the shopper to opt-in for digital FSIs and make a corporate commitment to reduce flyer size commensurately. In a world where digital has become the ultimate channel for any brand or retailer, empower and incentivize the consumer to drive m-CRM engagement.

M-SALES RACK: Likewise, soft goods retailers can offer VIP shopper sales. These store managers know that after the magic sixty-day mark, the chances of selling an item plummet to 15 percent. After ninety days, 5 percent. However, sales racks (distressed inventory) can be a loyalty driver. Have shoppers opt in for

a VIP mobile service that will inform them of deals based on their profiles. Mobile alerts trigger when tagged items in inventory are marked down.

M-SURVEY: This is my favorite m-bucket. It proves the simplicity and performance of mobilizing an existing channel. For a call center or PoS exit survey, try the following. Do not ask customers to remember to go to a website later that day to take a survey. Do not ask customers dialing through your call center to stay on the line for a survey. Ask them to take a one-minute *mobile survey* at their convenience. Text a survey asking:

Q	A
YES or NO	NO!
On a scale of 1–5	4
YES or NO	YES
Open-ended question	Liked their attitude

It takes just one minute *at the shopper's convenience*. For clients that run these services, customer satisfaction levels increase dramatically. If correctly incentivized, 5 percent to 30 percent of folk at the survey opt in—and 75 percent to 85 percent of the surveys are completed.

This rich two-way channel is allowing for more accurate shopper insights. As Tom Daly, head of mobile for Coca-Cola, says, "Mobile allows the brand to move from feedback *about* the consumers to become feedback *from* the consumers."

M-SPIFF: I personally like the m-spiff, as it is so simple. The brand incentivizes the retail sales clerk to opt in to a pop quiz to drive

product awareness on launches. The clerk simply texts to opt in to the "mobile university" and receives pop questions on products throughout the year.

> Is the new brand X printer
> 1. A
> 2. B
> 3. C
> Reply with the correct #. Reply STOP 2 exit BRANDX mobile university.

Loyalty points can be assigned for correct multiple-choice answers. The brand drives top-of-mind product knowledge and can reward the salesperson for caring enough to research correct responses to questions about the product.

M-SERVICE: So what about the blue shirts, the retail sales team? One consistent thread at every retail event that I have attended in the past year is the recommendation to provide a consistent technology experience between the store clerk and the shopper. Ironically, the modern shopper is better equipped than the clerk in many ways. Using the wireless network and a smartphone, the shopper can check and compare prices, and explore details of most products in the aisle. The clerk is challenged to perform simple merchandising inquiries.

To run an effective bricks-and-mortar business, the clerk and the shopper need to be aligned. Their devices need to speak the same language.

Be Your Own Cashier: Stop & Shop, Nordstrom, and Giant stores are running trials to let customers scan their products using

a scanner. Shoppers get targeted coupons and can see their check-out total. Kroger is exploring ways to provide handheld scanners to customers in the store that are identical to those used by the staff. The device can scan a product to allow for the shopper to shop and the staff person to sell more effectively. There are logistical issues in early trials; like self-service checkout lanes, this may be an inevitable but slow train coming.

Shaygan Kheradpir, chief operating officer of Barclays Global Retail Bank, talks about the "commercialization of IT." It is a good phrase to co-opt. You need to use the same screens in your stores as the shoppers' personal screens—their phones and tablets. Your blue shirts need to have smartphones, and your kiosks should feature tablets that will be familiar to most users.

In many ways, the store, which is battling the inevitable rise of large-screen Internet commerce, is now bringing the cloud inside its walls. The shopper is beginning to interface with the aisle as she is now accustomed to doing in the comfort of her home. Mobile is making this possible. Perhaps this is a happy medium for the future store. Providing the social setting for the shopper to navigate and touch tangible goods in the aisle but allowing for the control and convenience of the digital click.

According to an ARC Worldwide retail survey, shoppers consistently rate in-store service as weak. Shoppers want service to be relevant and to enhance the store, as opposed to just putting more people on the shop floor. Customers want help when they need it in order to *buy,* and they want to be left *alone* when they are in the self-directed *browsing* mode. Not only must the store be redesigned for this new navigation, so must store clerks be rethought to allow them to truly help digital shoppers.

M-PoS: Point of sale is a natural place to innovate. Square (with its 40 million pre-revenue valuation) lets plumbers to postmen take physical credit card payments with their Android or Apple phone using a free pocket-sized attachment that plugs into the audio jack socket. Anyone can accept a plastic card swipe: retail for the masses.

Mobile is enhancing existing services. PoS vendors such as SAP, Oracle, and Epicor Software Corporation are redesigning their point-of-sale software as a *point of engagement* for sales and mobile CRM. Middleware software companies like DigiPoS and Global Bay Mobile are designing black boxes to allow all store operations to appear on the clerk's or shopper's handheld.

Verifone's new PAYware device accepts every transaction variation the market has invented. It is a mobile mag stripe reader, PIN pad, NFC/contactless reader, bar code scanner—it slices, and it dices.

M-COUPON, M-RECEIPT: Mobile coupons and receipts are examples of how from end cap to aisle to checkout, the store is a-changing. Perhaps we should take a more critical look at that $50 billion spent on end cap.

Detailers of the world unite: less cardboard, more commerce!

Coupon Redux

The postrecession reality TV show *Extreme Couponing* follows coupon professionals who boast a 90 percent savings on their grocery bills. Meet two of the couponers: Tammilee Tillison lost her job the week of her wedding and had to find a way to survive for two, while Rebecca Davidson took a course at the YMCA with a local coupon blogger to get a better grasp on the basic skills involved in couponing. The shopper trend to supersave is growing.

According to Valassis, a leading retail media and marketing service, the economy is defining a new "normal" when it comes to shopping behavior. A whopping 94 percent of shoppers used consumer-packaged goods (CPG) coupons at least once in the past year, 77 percent used them regularly, and 30 percent said that they used more coupons than in the past. And more matched their shopping lists with coupons. Coupon redemption for grocery products increased by 25 percent over a twelve-month period. The economic downturn that began in 2008 made the coupon more attractive and more essential. The ten CPG categories with the highest growth are: paper and plastic products, packaged meat and seafood (refrigerated), candy and gum, coffee, yogurt, lightbulbs, electric goods and batteries, breakfast foods (frozen), salty snacks, laundry supplies, and pain relief medications (oral).

But the dog-eared coupon is not new to the corner store; it dates back to a pharmacist named John S. Pemberton, who created Coca-Cola in 1886. His first big challenge was to get people to try the new concoction. To promote the drink, he gave away handwritten chits for a free glass at local soda fountains. When the Great Depression hit in the 1930s, coupons began to ramp up, appearing in women's magazines and Sunday newspapers. The coupon industry boomed

in the fifties and sixties, as brands looked for a vehicle to launch new products and encourage consumers to give them a try.

The coupon had become an American birthright. In 1996, after over a hundred years of consumers clipping and saving, Procter & Gamble did the unthinkable and tested eliminating coupons from a major US market. Consumers actively boycotted P&G's products. The shopper had spoken, and the paper chits were now a necessary evil for brands.

Inmar, a large coupon clearinghouse, lists thirty-nine distribution channels for coupons, including direct mail, hospital samples, and the Internet. With all these options, the old-fashioned newspaper still accounts for a whopping 88.7 percent of coupon distribution. The targeted Internet drives a 4.33 percent coupon redemption indexing eight times higher than newspapers, but it accounts for only 0.3 percent of total distribution. The coupon is a very traditional medium. Trucks full of coupons roll across the border into Mexico every day for hand counting. The industry relies on this archaic system to settle the millions of dollars owed by the CPG (issuer) and the retailer (collector).

Archaic, maybe, but the system remains effective. Retailers know all too well that 80 percent of the products on the consumer's

shopping list is bought; however, the shopping list accounts for only 40 percent of their final basket. It seems that 60 percent of what gets piled in the basket comes from freestyle shopping and FMOT-ing. It is natural that with a mobile phone in almost every red-blooded American's pocket, there should be a few retailers trying to find ways to crack the mobile channel. Many believe that a factor in driving last-second decision making in the store could possibly be the new mobile coupon or mobile groupon. The traditional paper coupons provide 0.05 percent redemption. Mobile pundits are touting 20 percent to 40 percent higher rates than paper.

Bar Codes

Optimizing the store to drive incremental sales is nothing new. Back in 1948, Bernard Silver overheard a supermarket manager challenge the dean of his university to figure out how to capture product information automatically at checkout. Four years later, Silver was issued US Patent 2,612,994: the IP behind the retail bar code.

Silver proceeded to knock repeatedly on IBM's door with the idea. No luck. IBM said that reading the bar code information would require equipment that was way off in the future. Adoption was slow. The bar code, as we shoppers know, became the universal standard for retail information management. (I had a historic chuckle as I was walking in Chicago's O'Hare International Airport and saw an IBM retail solutions advertisement proudly showing a graphic of a retail bar code.)

Numbers like these make the average store manager weak in the knees. With chatter about the death of retail and the mall, and trends showing that shoppers are turning to new formats or are going online, how does the store manager keep the physical aisle relevant? How can new technology make shopping easier and more interactive?

We have the technology now to seamlessly scan a phone at the cash register and read a code that will tell us information to track coupons and vouchers. Four-fifths of all phones scan perfectly, and the one in five that do not are in India and China. Many digital scanning companies can demonstrate how a mobile phone displaying a code on the screen while spinning on a table can be scanned using an optical scanner with the optimized software. Mobile Houdini feats? Maybe, but it is clear that technology is not the barrier.

"It is a brave new world we are forecasting," says Mark Self, vice president of retail industry at Motorola Solutions. "The cell phone will open our house, car, track children, store loyalty points, cash. Technology is not the barrier. It is now in the hands of the retailer. The retailer needs to operationalize the mobile channel. Eventually—and I want to stress eventually—the cell phone will become the hub for everything. We are presently in the turf war. A fight for real estate."

Motorola Solutions (the sister company to the handset company that is now part of Google) is in the thick of this real estate war. It has much to gain from store upgrades to mobile-ready PoS. When JCPenney retrofitted its PoS for mobile trials, it switched out traditional laser scanners and dropped in new optical scanners that read through the phone's polarized coating. Target was just lucky. When the company upgraded its point of sale, it upgraded their scanners. It was only after this retrofit that Target discovered (much to the glee of the marketing folk) that it could use this hardware to scan a code on a phone.

Target proceeded to use this scanner to launch a mobile loyalty program. The consumer simply scans *one* 2-D code on his phone at checkout in the place of swiping a dog-eared loyalty card. Coupons are attached to this virtual card. Motorola has built a similar

mobile loyalty platform that allows retailers to mobilize their existing affinity cards and assign coupon offers.

"Retail behavior is slow to change," observes Mark Self. "It is an evolutionary process. Look at self-checkout: it took ten years to be adopted." The real challenge is not the technology but retail adoption. Many major retailers have legacy DOS-powered PoS. Hardware is equally antiquated. Can the retailer be coaxed into spending cash on upgrades? The Honeywell company sees a pickup in retail clients who are motivated to retrofit their point-of-sale terminal software and PoS scanners to "future proof" their stores for mobile coupon redemption.

Douglas G. Bergeron, the CEO of VeriFone, a major vendor of payment hardware in stores, warns that retailers will not retrofit for multiple bells and whistles. They will demand a unified PoS. "Retailers won't tolerate the need for multiple methods of acceptance to accommodate what will become a wide array of mobile-commerce schemes," he cautions. "All ideas, regardless of who generates them, must converge at a unified point of sale that is already integrated with other store systems and bank networks."

Three questions need to be answered:

- What m-coupon in-store solutions are available today?
- How can systems be integrated seamlessly?
- What are the logistical barriers to adoption?

For brands, coupons are often a necessary evil to drive product trial and conversion. Provisioning and clearing coupons is a costly exercise for a brand, and coupon clippers are fickle customers and are often *not* brand loyalists. (P&G today, Unilever tomorrow.) As

Alan Treadgold, retail head at ARC Worldwide, told an overflow crowd of retailers in Las Vegas at the annual GlobalShop retail conference, which attracts retailers from all across the United States looking for solutions for their stores, "Shoppers are promiscuous. Shoppers shop around. Loyalty needs to be won."

Redeeming coupons is the big expense: vendors wanting to implement a mobile redemption at the local grocery are warned to stay as far away as possible from the Byzantine contraption called point of sale. Glorified calculators full of custom code and black magic. Or, as the retail industry jokingly refers to it, an "abacus wrapped in plastic."

Catalina Marketing's checkout coupons have solved this by pure muscle, using external terminals to interface with the shopper. The amount of bubble gum and shoestring that has been used to avoid dealing with the retail chief information officer is mind-boggling.

Ultimately, the cost and inefficiencies of coupons and tracking discounts foster an air of mistrust between retailer (big box) and manufacturer (the box).

Paper coupons are by no means a precise science.

1. **OVERREACH**: paper does not allow for the limitless need for targeting and segmentation.
2. **WRONG SHOPPER**: spend money speaking to shoppers that would possibly buy the product without the discount.
3. **WRONG TIMING**: not engaging with the consumer at the moment of decision making.

Recommended Reading:
NRF Mobile Retailing Blueprint

The Association for Retail Technology Standards (ARTS), a division of the National Retail Federation (NRF), spent about a year writing the *NRF Mobile Retailing Blueprint,* a document that describes the mobile landscape for the retail industry. About fifty subject matter experts, including five additional standards organizations, worked together to write about mobile marketing, mobile commerce, mobile payment, and mobile operations. It's a great document for retailers to review so they can see the types of applications on the market and the different implementation options (http://blogs.oracle.com /retail/2010/07/nrf_mobile_retailing_blueprint.html). The next step for ARTS is to determine where standards need to be created, and then organize the stakeholders.

But times are changing. A few things are happening to advance paperless coupons. In addition to every shopper having a phone in her bag along with her store loyalty card and wallet, the PoS is finally moving from *point of sale* to *point of service,* with more network smarts.

As a service, the PoS is developing the networked ability to run value-added third-party content, channels, and services. Requirements such as loyalty programs have pushed the CIO to deploy centrally across the enterprise, and the Association for Retail Technology Standards is quarterbacking this with global standards. (See box above.)

Redemption is the key consideration. To be an effective substitute for paper and plastic, we need to resolve authentication and fraud prevention. If you simply put a generic promotional bar code on a mobile, there is little to stop a consumer from copying the code and posting it on Facebook. The coupons and vouchers must be authenticated uniquely against a centralized clearinghouse to stop

fraud and malredemption. A manufacturer would not be amused to receive a bill for $100 million from a retailer on a promotional campaign without data or evidence.

The question, then, is, How can the phone interface with the PoS to allow for seamless, trackable redemption? There are six main approaches:

1. TXT-BASED COUPON

American Eagle Outfitters sends a two-digit code to the consumer via SMS, and the consumer quotes this at checkout for the promotional discount. Any longer code would become a logistical issue to enter at PoS. Manual entry slows down the line.

A two-digit code cannot be tracked back to the consumer. It is not really a coupon but more of an "offer," as it is not tracked from provisioning to redemption. It cannot be audited by a third party. This is not workable for P&G coupons in, say, Safeway, where a clearinghouse needs to count and validate coupons to make sure all parties pay and are paid for a given promotion.

2. CODE-BASED COUPON

While code scanning is a good solution, there is a need for image scanners on each aisle, staff training, and the danger of slowing down the aisle on single and multiple coupon redemption. Additionally, mobile coupon redemption is fraught with logistical problems:

- **"Sorry, waiting for a connection."** Coupons need to be pre-loaded, as Internet speed and connection are not a 100 percent given at checkout.

 Solution: network bandwidth and reach magically improve, or the retailer opens a Wi-Fi network for its shopper community.

- "Oh, I have one more to scan . . ." Multiple codes slow down the aisle.

 Solution: use one code and consolidate offers to that account.

- "Oops, I dropped your phone!" Clerks will instinctively handle the consumers' phone to gun accurately.

 Solution: provide self-scanning at PoS and focus initial pilots at self-checkout.

The grocery store shopper uses multiple offers, and the aisle needs to move quickly. For this reason, mobile coupon implementations with Kroger and Safeway are not likely to use code-based in-aisle code scanning any time soon. For this reason, I would encourage any retailer to look to the self-checkout line as an ideal place to install self-scan m-coupon redemption terminals.

3. KIOSK REDEMPTION

Don't like scanning at checkout? Let the shopper do your dirty work at a kiosk. The store or brand opts consumers into deal alerts and sends them mobile coupon codes that can be scanned at the multidirectional optical scanner built into the kiosk. The unit then spits out a good old paper coupon for the aisle. This is using mobile to drive "last mile" and paper on the "final foot."

4. PIN PAD REDEMPTION

The family-owned Meijer regional grocery chain, with roughly two hundred superstores, has launched an mPerks system. Jeff Handler, senior vice president of marketing and advertising, has thrown out all the mobile moving parts and simply attached online and store marketing to the phone number. With mPerks, the

shopper intuitively enters his or her phone number at checkout as a unique ID. Offers are bundled.

Steven Rothwell in Surrey, England, has built Eagle Eye around a global patent on tying the coupon or voucher to the phone number. The coupons and vouchers are redeemed at checkout when the consumer keys a PIN on the PIN pad. Steve is confident that US shoppers will adopt this solution. However, until chip-and-PIN terminals are more common in the United States and the retailer is willing to move outside their traditional loyal card swipe, adoption may be slow.

5. MOBILE CLIPPING TO LOYALTY CARD

The US retail market has done an effective job in assigning numbers to shoppers. A loyalty number allows for affinity programs and shopping rewards for shop loyalists. There are holes in the market, with Wal-Mart being the "everyday low prices" gorilla. But many of the dominant retail players have carded the consumer.

These cards can be used effectively for digital coupon redemption or electronic proof of purchase (EPP). Most of these are e-coupons clipped from online discount portals. Many brands question the value and cost of digital clipping, as companies such as Coupons.com are billing for digital "distribution," when the consumer simply checks the box online to tether this value to his or her loyalty card. If the consumer is doing this "just-in-case," she may buy an item regardless and the coupon is not driving the in-store sale.

From the brand's perspective, the optimal scenario is for the impulse shopper to coupon-clip in-aisle. This directly affects the shopping behavior. YOU Technology is leading the charge in on-demand clipping to a stored-value card. The shopper can SMS an offer while in the aisle and instantly have the coupon assigned to

his or her loyalty card. (This directly impacts the shopping decision in the five-foot-by-five-seconds box.)

American Express's partnership with Facebook is a good example of effectively appending virtual coupons to an existing card. Consumers can select offers and tether these deals to their AmEx card. The beauty of this solution is that it is riding existing commerce rails. American Express's "Link, Like, Love" solution will offer targeted deals across multiple retailers nationally, and, most important, it is ready for prime time today.

6. NEAR FIELD COMMUNICATION (NFC)

Finally, there is the ability to provide fluid integration with mobile payment terminals using near field communication, or machine-to-machine short-range wireless connectivity. The proximity payment solution can also deliver coupons and loyalty communications.

Google deals auto-synchronize to the m-Wallet. These could be discounts that the shopper clicks via a Google search ad or opts in to a (Groupon-like) "deal of the day."

While this is unquestionably the smart solution in the long term (as it integrates seamlessly with the mobile wallet and the proximity payment, providing content to the consumer and speed at PoS to the retailer), it is available only at participating merchants. The time line for ubiquitous NFC adoption, as discussed earlier, is a moving target.

Wow, that is a confusing array of options! If you think you are flummoxed, imagine the poor shopkeeper. Mark Self from Motorola wisely reminded me of the famous economist John Maynard Keynes's words during the Great Depression:

We need solutions *now* because "in the long run, we are all dead."

Things to Consider: The Male Coupon Clipper?

While women lead the charge when it comes to clipping coupons, more than half the guys in the United States have smartphones. According to a 2010 survey of consumer habits from InsightExpress, men actually overindexed in coupon usage at least at certain types of stores:

electronics store—30 percent (general population, 10 percent);
clothing store—33 percent (general population, 15 percent);
department store—30 percent (general population, 15 percent);
service location—16 percent (general population, 7 percent).

They are more inclined to go hunting for coupons. When InsightExpress asked preference for receiving mobile coupons, 51 percent said they would prefer to find coupons themselves via an application, compared to just 28 percent of the general population; 39 percent said they wanted to text in to receive them at the store, as opposed to 27 percent of the general population.

Things to Consider: The Store

Most stores have point-of-sale limitations that need to be considered when designing any program that requires coupon or offer redemption and tracking. Take most fast-food restaurants: their point of sale is unlikely networked, and coupons are often difficult to track.

1. Although the PoS can be customized for offers, the store owner needs to input these into the system manually and rarely will do this.
2. In many cases, store managers will refuse certain corporate offers if they are difficult to manage.

3. In most cases, the cost of any discount is borne by the store and not passed on to corporate.

If the store accepts a coupon, the staff will usually trigger the discount with a generic discount key:

```
              QUIZNOS #6801

   ORDER  #  01132

       RG MESQUITI              6.99
       $ DISCOUNT              -1.00

    TAKE-OUT

                        $      5.99
       TAX TOTAL        $      0.78
       TOTAL            $      6.77

       CASH             $      6.77

   3780        COUNTER      AUG.22,2011
               REG1-AM         12:46

      Customer comments call 866-4TOASTED
        Visit us at www.quiznos.com
```

Many stores will not be able to or want to use an image scanner to scan a phone. Essentially, the phone needs to emulate the business logic of the existing store behavior and therefore needs to be treated as a nonunique code or multiple-use code.

In this case, the coupon is simply an offer sent to the phone, and the phone is simply a way of displaying the offer.

The Mighty Mobile PIN

I am a great believer in the humble mobile PIN. It has done mobile a huge service, starting with the first PIN promotions run in Europe in 2002. That same year, I flew to Munich, Germany, to meet with Dr. Michael Birkel, the founder of 12Snap (or, in German, *Eins Zwei* Snap). Originally a dot-bomb online auctioning company, it reinvented itself as one of the first mobile marketers on the

planet, along with Flytxt and Mindmatics. The industry owes all three much thanks.

At the end of Birkel's Mobile Marketing 101 slide deck, I was rewarded with a Cadbury Crunchie candy bar and a McDonald's large-sized French fries container to bring back to the US. The candy bar had a large starburst advertising a unique PIN-in-pack for a chance to win £1 million: "TXT2CIFURAWINR." I kept this candy bar in my computer bag for three years, hauling it to hundreds of brand meetings until the chocolate and caramel had ossified. Only the crumpled wrapper remains in my office.

The Cadbury promotion was very successful and very simple: buy me and win. (Pure *Willy Wonka* golden ticket.) The consumer will respond to the Pavlovian jingle of a unique PIN on product

if there is a chance to win stuff. If the PIN is *unique* and *proof of purchase,* the consumer sees this as a reward. Conversely, if the consumer views the PIN as generic, then the value diminishes, and the motivation for redeeming the PIN or paying attention to it is reduced commensurately.

In retail terms, the value of a product is the worth a shopper assigns to it. The product's perceived benefit in relation to the perceived costs is often expressed as the following equation:

$$\text{Value} = \text{Benefits} / \text{Cost}$$

How do we make a similar shopper equation for "value" on a promotional level? In the world of mobile promotion, the PIN is the reward or value.

- **PIN VALUE**: The shopper will imbue the PIN with value if it comes from an action or transaction the shopper has made. Consumers know intuitively that they get nothing for nothing. There needs to be a trade-off or exchange of value to receive a reward.
- **PIN UNIQUENESS**: The reward needs to be clearly shown to be a unique reward for this action. You cannot put a generic PIN on the collateral, as this is instantly seen as a dupe and not acted on.

The consumer needs to feel that the PIN is unique to her and has been assigned as a fair exchange for something that she did to earn it. Tying a dynamic PIN to a shopper transaction will make the shopper attribute more value to this PIN. Conversely, tying a *non*unique PIN to a transaction—or, worse yet, throwing a PIN

on a highway billboard—will immediately diminish the shopper's incentive to redeem or take action based on this PIN.

For lack of a more scientific reference for value assigned to mobile PINs, I will call this the "Click-to-*ka-ching!*" rule:

PIN Value = Reward / Uniqueness

The perceived value of the PIN is *lower* if the reward is triggered via a *non*unique PIN, while the perceived value of the PIN is *higher* if the reward is triggered via a unique PIN.

The shopper demands a fair exchange: put a unique PIN inside a candy bar or on a Subway sandwich and watch sales go up by 15 percent to 30 percent.

This is powerful stuff. Retailers know that it requires a 40 percent plus discount to move a shopper from her existing brand. The small value assigned to a PIN will keep her loyal.

Give Rewards More Credit

Coca-Cola has taken this in-store strategy to the next level. The Atlanta-based company has successfully turned its classic Coke bottle into a mini–retail environment to run affinity direct-to-consumer (D2C) programs. Coke prints a unique promotional PIN,

or alphanumeric code, on the underside of the bottle cap; this serves as proof of purchase on specially marked Coca-Cola products and on special promotional materials that can be redeemed via mobile and online. Coke's program works as an affinity channel in any store, allowing the consumer to text message the PINs to collect rewards points. Everyone who texts a PIN code receives a number of iCoke Points. The consumers work diligently to accumulate points to redeem against tickets and other valued swag.

The style guide for the first Coca-Cola mobile PIN on product in 2006. "Sign Up, Enter Codes, Collect Points"—It all starts under the cap.

Coca-Cola has taken this token to the ultimate mobile exchange in France, United Kingdom, and Canada, where "Coke Points" can be instantly redeemed for instant wireless minutes. TXT and instantly get wireless money.

There is an instant rebate: cash in hand for the mobile consumer. It's the dream commerce exchange: redeem loyalty points on your handset, and the brand will top up minutes on the same redemption device. Coke is using the phone as retailers use a plastic loyalty card. The value exchange can be moved seamlessly on and off the card (or in this case, phone). There are no time delays or intermediaries between the brand and the shopper.

PIN Problems?

All of the above exciting promotional options depend upon tethering unique PINs to a product or purchase. The problem with PINs is that they are logistically difficult and operation intensive to print, sticker, and attach to a product. NFC tags can be tapped through the product and do not act as proof of purchase.

Just try to have a marketing genius walk into the brand's operations department and ask to have unique PINs printed somewhere on a product (invisible to the consumer until after purchase) that is about to be shipped nationally! Outside of the legal machinations on the PIN patents in market, and outside of the ink and printing quandary, operations folk now need to consider how they will manage a campaign that may have an end date. The promotional products with active PINs will sit on the shelf of multiple stores for an undetermined period of time long after the campaign ends.

Bottom line: if you can do it, do it! If you can't, here is another option.

The market needs to work on a way of taking the pain of PIN provisioning off the table. If the PIN is not printed on the product, what else is proof of purchase? Where the PIN-in-product is proof of purchase (or, as I affectionately like to say, is proof of theft), the ultimate proof of purchase are the point-of-sale data on a *loyalty card* or physically on the *receipt*.

That being the case, there are only two options, and they are both (much to the chagrin of the manufacturer) at retail checkout.

One is automated electronic proof of purchase integrated with a loyalty card. EPP can be used to digitally track coupons and wireless rebates off the shopper's loyalty card based on purchase behavior. This is an option for a store that has a loyalty system in place with some integrated mobile CRM system or list man-

agement. The item purchased and the loyalty identification are matched, and mobile rewards can be sent to the user based on his or her purchase behavior. If there is an existing mobile opt-in, SMS can be sent to the shopper, advising her of the credit reward after a single purchase or based on a group of products bought. The retailer can allow for breakage by requesting that the shoppers respond to the SMS for a credit to be triggered.

The other is to use the receipt . . .

Get a Receipt!

The receipt is one of the most valued and underutilized retail inventions. The history of the receipt starts with a disgruntled Ohio restaurateur named James Ritty, who reportedly had a nervous breakdown from all his employee theft. Ritty took a convalescent cruise to Europe and on the way invented the first cash register, which he called the "Ritty's Incorruptible Cashier."

Ritty built a number of models but hardly managed to sell one unit. Fortunately for receipts, one of the machines he did sell was to John Henry Patterson, then the owner of a small coal business, who went on to found the National Cash Register company. Ritty's focus was on solving fraud. Patterson expanded the role of the register from a cash container and basic calculator into a marketing tool. NCR first started selling registers capable of printing receipts—or checks, as they were known—in 1893.

But Patterson knew that no innovation is worth anything without adoption. He needed to change the behavior of the shopper who had never received anything from the register outside of the change and the *ka-ching!* of the transaction bell at checkout (which, by the way, NCR patented). Patterson ran a "Get a receipt" campaign to

shoppers, highlighting the services they should expect from the businesses they patronized. He was so committed to this campaign tagline that he inscribed it on his personal travel truck.

The receipt won a place in American shopping because it struck a utilitarian cord with the consumer. But the receipt's function has not profoundly evolved over the past one hunded years. Early on, NCR understood the value of this piece of paper that found its way into nearly every consumer's wallet. The company encouraged businesses to use receipts as ways to advertise and encourage repeat business through rebates using receipts and even contests using specially marked receipts.

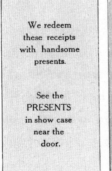

We redeem these receipts with handsome presents.

See the PRESENTS in show case near the door.

4 2 9 6 APR 25

★B - 0.50

MEYER & HOLT
806 Pine St.

Return $10 in cash receipts like this and get $11 worth of trading stamps.

In Patterson's 1912 brochure promoting the service to retailers, the product guide states, "The N.C.R. 'Get a Receipt' plan is quick and efficient. At the time the record is made on the register, the receipt is automatically printed and issued . . . [the] receipt furnishes valuable advertising . . . This is the most direct form of advertising known."

In spite of this shopper insight, the receipt remained largely underutilized. The bottom of most retail receipts has a static "Have a nice day!" message. Marketing companies print coupons on the back of the receipt. Survey companies put generic PINs on the receipt for online data collection. Redemption rates are low because:

1. The click-to-*ka-ching!* rule makes this low perceived value.
2. You're forcing the consumer to go to a distant interactive destination to redeem.

But the receipt is far more than a mere record of purchase. It can be easily transformed into more valuable currency by giving it a promotional value. The receipt can be recast as a "lottery ticket" or a "scratch and win." The receipt can emulate Coca-Cola's success with PIN-under-cap by placing unique PINs on the receipt based on what the consumer buys. The receipt can drive the same affinity goals without changing packaging. Moreover, by intelligently looking at the consumer basket as tender, PINs can trigger surveys and analytics that are gold to any retailers and CPG.

"Buy my product and check your receipt to win."

Nine in ten bank ATM and retail PoS receipts are trashed or never get removed from the bottom of the wallet or bag. If this piece of paper is consistently given a promotional value based on the shopper's transactions, he or she will attribute value. Call it a

"virtual scratch and win" and have it constantly on all receipts. The mobile consumer will respond.

The PIN on the receipt becomes the proof of purchase and redemption on any incentive happening post-transaction and post-PoS on the consumer's phone. Using the receipt as a scratch-and-win solves the two most critical problems that the retailer faces: (1) targeted sales (with little lead time), and (2) one-to-one CRM (via consumer opt-in).

In South Africa, retail trials are in place to tie the PIN redemption to wireless airtime rewards. Coupon value is instantly redeemed in wireless airtime cash value. This "instant rebate" eliminates the need for coupon clearinghouses and the painful time lapse on coupon settlement. Amazingly, the shopper is doing all the work.

```
========================
     FREELOAD COUPON
      SERIAL NO.206211
  COUPON PIN VALUE  r.5.00
           DIAL.
  *130 *789 * PIN. NO. #PRESS

     PIN.: 761 224 265 631
     PIN.: 761 298 233 763
     PIN.: 761 169 463 872

 . Valid for Vodacom, MTN, Cell C. Prepaid phones
 . Will reload within minutes & be confirmed
 . A FREELOAD is TOTALLY FREE with no Cost to reload

  FOR HELP DIAL 0800 00 6569
       www.freeload.co.za
```

In the United States, PoS vendors are leveraging basket intelligence to assign PIN on *receipt* to drive SMS instant promotions, instant surveys, and, of course, capture a relationship with the consumer's mobile number postcheckout.

More important, the solution does not slow down the aisle or require the retail clerk to do anything beyond business as usual. Fraud is unlikely (unless the clerk pockets the receipt in front of the client's face), and we are entering into a mobile relationship with every participating shopper.

A Perfect Retail Storm

These options do not kick PIN-on-product promotions to the curb. The brand will always opt for a direct relationship with the shopper if it has a choice. However, dynamic electronic proof of purchase (EPP integration or SMS PINs on receipts) offers powerful ROI on ROI-challenged services such as:

- Surveys: These historically have abysmally low redemption because the PIN is generic (low perceived value), and the redemption is far away online.
- End-of-aisle promotions: measured end-to-end conversion off the $50 billion spent on paper and plastic.
- Rebates: the ability to drive rewards without discounting the product, eliminating traditional clearinghouses and collecting valuable mobile CRM.

The future of receipt integration just gets stickier: Forrester Research, a technology and market research company, indicates that the evolution of the paper receipt is digital, seeming to predict that ultimately all engagement will be directly with the consumer's phone.

7 ADVERTISING ON THE COMMERCE CHANNEL

In nine years of agency pizza lunches, industry panels, and client presentations, the pitch was always mobile engagement. With Nielsen graphs showing mobile adoption rocketing into the twenteens, mobile marketers razzled and dazzled the poor media planners. For every lunch-and-learn pizza slice they ate, we made them listen to the mantra: "Mobile can activate your traditional media. Run a mobile campaign."

In those formative days, everything was about trial. Few of these mobile services had key performance indicators (KPIs) attached, and most had a start-and-stop date with zero sense of continuity or integration into the larger brand plan.

When mobile was grudgingly added by the creative agency, the media agency relegated it to a tiny copyright-size call to action. Inevitably, the campaign failed because no one outside the account manager knew it existed.

Few made any money, and the best of the mobile technology companies were stooged into becoming agency support shops or, worse yet, "mobile agencies" to drive adoption in the market.

Then the industry matured (a little). We started discussing a two-step pitch: acquisition and retention. Even without pizza graft, agencies and brands started to ask, "How do we get the mobile consumer, and how do we hold on to them?"

Agencies started to see mobile as an extension of their affinity, loyalty, and CRM programs. Mobile was less stand-alone and more "let me see your APIs." Coke and other iconic brands started to seamlessly integrate their existing affinity strategy to SMS and mobile web. Suddenly mobile had more buy-in and stickiness across multiple touch points and channels.

Then the recession hit in 2008, and media planning went into rigor mortis. The digital slice, which had grown steadily to 20 percent of the buy, stalled, and the surrounding 80 percent of the traditional pie started to shrink. Consumers lost their will to spend, and retailers either hid under the desk or began to think outside of business as usual.

I think, by and large, that this navel-gazing period was incredibly productive. I remember flying from the annual IAB summit in Orlando, Florida, straight to the Retail Advertising and Marketing Association's annual conference in Las Vegas, listening to one speaker after another begin with PowerPoint slides showing spiraling graphs, and pundits drawing Wall Street–Madison Avenue parallels. What was abundantly clear was that Main Street and Madison Avenue were at a crossroad. How to reengage the consumer? How to reengage return on investment (ROI)?

With the recession abating somewhat, the campaign economy has changed yet again. Companies that for years branded themselves as "mobile marketing agencies" or "mobile marketing technology shops" have suddenly rebranded their wares as "mobile commerce."

Now the pitch is acquisition to drive the consumer to some tangible return on advertising (ROA). Every second article on mobile is

about couponing, m-commerce, or m-ticketing. The focus has become closed-loop programs that can end in some form of conversion.

Suddenly we are talking about measuring beyond the advertising click, or what the industry calls attribution analytics. The market has matured (God bless it) into acquisition, conversion, retention: discover the customer, do something with him or her that will end in a transaction of some kind, and then work out a way of holding on for dear life.

Point of sale, m-commerce, and m-couponing are all now topics of most brand meetings. Understanding the mobile consumer and how this consumer transacts on the phone is key to developing a mobile strategy.

Mobile Mouse

About three years ago, I wrote an article titled "There Is No Such Thing as a Mobile Campaign," in the *Mobile Marketer*. Readers may have quietly gasped and hurriedly moved on to the next article, but it seemed to strike a chord. Look around. The world continues to buy media vertically. (TV, radio, print, and even online are farmed out to the digital agency and bought as a segmented buy.) If you run mobile as a stand-alone campaign, it is doomed to the graveyard of Yes-I-tried mobile case studies.

Mobile is an integrated part of the buy and would not exist, in most cases, without a 360-degree plan. Why? Mobile is primarily a pull media. It needs to be added to the traditional push media to come to life and work its magic.

The most touted example of mobile pull is when the brand uses the phone as a mobile mouse and the short code as the mobile click to activate its media.

Concert promoters Live Nation and AEG Live leverage their

digital display boards and drive the concertgoer to the sponsor's intended destination, far beyond the venue. Using mobile sweeps, PINs, and coupons as incentives, mobile works to engage and bridge the consumer to high-ROI destinations.

Coca-Cola's PIN-on-product mobile affinity program has no start date or end date; just a continual channel that turns the phone into a reward card permitting consumers to add points to their account as they leave the convenience store.

Why are these approaches to mobile effective? Because all of the above examples are not run as one-off campaigns but as an always-on cross-media channel. Mobile is an interactive pull element that helps these media clients dialogue with their consumer. It is an always-on element of the media mix, and it connects media dots that historically never dialogued.

The same holds true for good mobile multiscreen engagement. Simply incorporating a mobile opt-in form on the larger-screen web "sign-up page" to allow for targeted handset alerts can be powerful tool for the brand.

Avoiding Cross-Channel Disconnect

A recent Forrester consumer survey found that more than half of consumers buying in bricks-and-mortar begin their research process online. Cross-channel shopping is expected to top $1 trillion

by 2012. Although consumers are actively cross-channel shopping for their considered purchases, brands and retailers fail to create a seamless multichannel shopping experience.

Microsoft refers to this as the "multiscreen multiplier": each screen multiplies the brand value, resulting in a measured ROA across all the channels. Brand managers are trying their best to understand how to leverage all the screens and keep their messaging and goals constant on television, gaming, online, and mobile real estate.

But shoppers are way ahead of us simple media folk: they are channel agnostics. While the media planner continues to buy media vertically, mobile is one of the only media elements that can help the consumer move from the dress on the billboard, to the dress online, to the dress in the aisle.

So in a world of vertical buying, mobile is a horizontal; it effectively helps the planner connect the dots. And in connecting the brand's media touch points, it drives incremental value on the vertical buy by aiding measurability and accountability, but, more important, by helping move the consumer from the ad placement to where the brand needs her to be: at the point of sale, online store:

Mobile is a horizontal buy that adds value to your vertical push media.

- Activate traditional publishing mediums.
- Create a permission-based two-way channel.
- Help the brand bridge to PoS, web, CRM programs.

If media planners continue to see mobile as an independent campaign that is not designed specifically to bridge consumers, then they are missing the value of the mobile channel, and mobile will inevitably not drive ROI in the 360-degree media plan, ending up as a media also-ran.

It struck me after eight years in the mobile marketing world that I can safely say that it is as complex and fragile as any ecosystem. It is difficult to find a levelheaded voice to help explain how all the pieces fit together.

On the contrary, we are faced with mobile evangelists who travel through town with a loud bell touting one or two isolated services. What is for sale today? NFC, bluetooth, mobile augmented reality, m-coupon scanning at retail point of sale, and so on. Unfortunately, solution-driven strategies rarely work. What does?

Discovery

Let's starts at the bottom of the food chain. I would guess that the mobile food chain begins with discovery. Mobile, unlike push media and even online media (that has better search ergonomics), is not something the consumer can find easily. Without a well-planned discovery strategy, mobile is vanity press and simply does not exist. We have discussed the importance of SMS in mobile discovery and engagement; however, there are many channels that the retailer can leverage for in-store and on-media discovery:

QR CODES: We have discussed the value and limitations of using 2-D codes in retail to drive discovery. While scanning codes can be an effective way of driving the shopper into a deeper mobile-web engagement, unless you scan-to-text or scan-to-talk (as discussed earlier), the click-through is anonymous and is not a two-way channel.

TWITTER: Often confused as a discovery media, Twitter is compared with SMS because of its SMS-like character-length messages. Bryce Marshall, former director of strategic services at Focus.com, explains in a wonderfully succinct way that Twitter has a specific utility: microblogging. Tweeting is a "phenomenon unto itself and does not need—or deserve—to be muddled in the definition of mobile."

Twitter is not direct digital marketing. Its followers are fans and loyalists but it has no targeted CRM, no ability to activate other channels to seamlessly move the fan or loyalist to bricks-and-mortar or m-commerce destinations. Marshall explains that this activation channel is the domain of the opt-in SMS database that can be effectively refined, targeted, and activated. Opt-in SMS allows for a two-way communication that can guide and refine the impulse consumer's decision making.

Yes, the brand can follow the follower and, through this reciprocal channel, send private two-way messages, but this is not straightforward for a consumer to understand—and definitely not how the social-media tool was designed. It is a 5/8-inch socket wrench, a specialized tool to build a grassroots advocate network that allows followers to redistribute dialogue through one-click retweets, says Marshall.

"In comparison, well-designed opt-in SMS marketing pro-

grams provide not just offers or notifications of sales events but also can automate valuable services, such as providing information on store locations and driving directions, execute delivery and shipping status alerts, provide reminders on bank balances, send alerts when out-of-stock items are now in stock, or help online shoppers get in-store help with a purchase decision. All of these services—and more—are provided through a comprehensive SMS marketing approach that delivers extraordinary value and brand experiences for customers."

BLUETOOTH: Here we have another channel that is often associated with retail engagement. Similar to a tweet, this is a one-way channel. The biggest challenge is that most handsets on the market are not turned on for inbound Bluetooth messaging. And for the few handsets that are turned on for Bluetooth, the message is targeted only by general location, and the content can be easily construed negatively by the shopper as spam.

NFC: As near field communication enables phones to enter the market, tap-to-activate solutions will become more pervasive. Simply tagging a product or media with an RFID tag will allow for proximity activation. The consumer taps his or her phone on an NFC call to action, and this can open the browser, deliver a coupon, or bridge to a multitude of other services such as location, talk, and payment.

Look to stores, products, and even books to become tapable, allowing this physical real estate to function as a mobile bridge to a digital purchase. The national chain GameStop is allowing customers to download games in its stores, products are bundling RFID tags to help close sales, and even this book may be a tap-to-try, tap-to-buy experience for Simon & Schuster.

Activation

Peter Vesterbacka, founder of Rovio (creator of the game Angry Birds), explains that mobile is about the experience, saying, "You would not play audio-only media on a television. Any advertising in Angry Birds needs to cater to the mobile experience. Be interactive."

He is correct. "Mobile interactive" is a fundamentally different animal from its related genus, "online interactive." Although a click is a click is a click, and thus follows many of the online or large-screen characteristics, there are two key differences:

1. **GEOGRAPHY**: The mobile primate is "mobile" and therefore closer to where her brand sponsor would like her to be: at the mall, convenience store, dealership, event, and so forth.
2. **CONSUMPTION**: Mobile is on-the-run snack food, whereas online is a sit-down meal. As my colleague at the IAB, Joe Laszlo, explains, the mobile consumer uses the phone to "save time"—perhaps looking up an address or a location

on a digital map—or to "kill time," filling unexpected slow moments in the day. (This use case, too, is likely to be short and interrupted unexpectedly; however, a user in this mode is open to—indeed, hoping for—amusing distractions.)

The mobile user is often consuming in a quick, impulsive manner, and therefore it is an ideal environment to opt in to savings alerts, coupons, promotions, store reminders, and so on. And because these offers are consumed on the run, the mobile user is often ideally positioned to act on a call to action.

With this in mind, mobile cannot be just about impression-based advertising but must extend beyond-the-click activation and bridge to point of sale, point of entry, and so forth. The brand misses half the mobile ecosystem if consumers do not explore past the mobile display.

Mobile is all about "what's next."

iRevenue

When Google bought the mobile advertising network AdMob in 2009, the market was eagerly awaiting the positive fallout. Then Apple acquired the Quattro Wireless Network's mobile ad network (for a modest quarter-billion dollars) and closed it down a few months later.

I wrote then that maybe it would be overly simplistic or apologetic to say that up until the billion-dollar drop, we were all just building a network and waiting. Well, it seems we are still waiting.

Where are we in making mobile into a healthy media buy? When someone uploads another YouTube video that generates more ad inventory, it creates a glut of consumer impressions. Does

this drive down the value of the impression? Not really. It is not about the impression as much as the "attention." Advertising impressions may not be scarce but advertising "attention" is scarce and in high demand.

Mobile nose-to-phone attention can provide huge value to certain consumer brands and retailers. With many publishers bundling the mobile buy free or discounted with a more robust online commitment, it is difficult to explain to the buyer the unique and powerful value of the mobile CPM (cost per thousand consumer impressions).

Speak with media planners, and they will tell you the following about mobile inventory buying:

1. For a small wedge of the digital buy, it is "mighty hard to buy."
2. The CPM "seems too high for the value add."
3. To drive an integrated buy with postclick strategy, there are "too many moving parts."

The Interactive Advertising Bureau has worked hard to demystify the buy by publishing a *Mobile Buyer's Guide* that holds the media planner's hand as he extends his digital buy to mobile. However, no guide will drive significant dollars into mobile until the mobile buy is not an also-ran to the online buy and commands a respectable CPM in its own right.

History Repeats Itself

The nice thing about any mobile debate is that we have inevitably gone through the same issue historically with other emerging media channels.

Remember how mainstream television sold specialty channels? The value proposition made sense: programming targeted at a specific demographic. The inventory was in many cases bundled as a package deal for some unsuspecting brand.

When the online buy appeared in the mid-1990s, sales teams grudgingly added it as a sweetener to the television's thirty-second advertisement buy. It was free stuff—no one sold it, and no one knew how—but it was part of the bundle: what publishers called "share of voice."

Rinse and repeat. The online sales team is now a mature powerhouse. Hell, it is the only team selling in this new economy. Finally, we have conceded that analog dollars are moving to digital dimes. Traditional media is losing its brand loyalists.

Take the "local real estate agent" test. Look around at local media content:

- Ten years ago, your local real estate broker was advertising on the placard behind the park bench.
- Five years ago, she was advertising on the bus shelter.
- Today she can afford a billboard!

We now have a media that is targeted and measured. Apart from a dwindling legacy of thirty-minute-spot executives golfing with big brands, the world has changed.

A few online sales people are now tasked with selling mobile impressions. Again, a generation gap. Mobile is bundled with the online buy. No one can explain the mobile value proposition well. Indeed, it becomes more difficult than it is "worth" to become a resident expert.

The Native Mobile Salesperson

For mobile to be sold effectively, two things have to happen:

1. *Take online CPMs for a walk.* Mobile needs to be treated as business as usual, with similar vernacular and measurement standards as other digital buys. The Interactive Advertising Bureau and the Mobile Marketing Association, with the guidance of George Ivie of the Media Rating Council, are making great strides in this direction. The buyer is now able to compare online and mobile measurement guidelines and have comfort in consistency.
2. *Mobile creative ad units.* At the same time, the industry needs to present the planner/buyer with creative ad units that drive engagement and postclick conversion that is unique to the mobile channel.

The mobile community has worked hard to develop creative ad units that are native to mobile. Before Quattro was eaten and spat out by Apple, it started to develop innovative interactive ads that were expanded into a more comprehensive Apple "iAd" strategy. Apple touted its iAd as delivering all the emotion and movement of *TV ads* with the interactivity of *web ads*. The bang is delivered by HTML5 magic inside the application. (For this sensory experience, Apple will iSell and iServe the ads, and developers will receive a large chunk of the iRevenue.)

iAd had a lot of hype out of the gate. But as the dust settles, there is more than the PR piece that brands need to take into account in a media buy. The iAd promised emotional connection, continuity, and interactivity inside the APP, and brands seem willing to pay a pretty penny for this value.

But if Apple is only 20 percent of the ad inventory fill, and you need to throw out the creative that your $300,000 art director has designed for 80 percent of your campaign inventory to work with the Apple team, then many planners are going to think twice about investing too heavily in iAd units. iAd is designed for iRevenue and is not industry agnostic. Mobile buying is hard enough without this complexity. (Ask Adidas, which took its initial $10 million budget elsewhere.)

But the opportunity goes beyond these innovative units.

Hone Phone

Presently, these creative ad units are helping mobile deliver contextual and targeted messaging with location, carrier profile, and self-selection. They also help measure the quality and duration of engagement.

Ad network owners are developing more refined targeting data to drive up the value of their networks. The Jumptap ad network correlates anonymous browsing history and location to attempt to target the ad to the consumer in order to enhance the value of their ad inventory. Information is profiled and coupled to mobile ad units that are served dynamically.

"What I recall from my days running the Excite Internet portal back in 1997 is that customers found messaging 'Big Brotherish' when it appeared to be irrelevant," says George Bell, Jumptap's CEO. "Mobile is ten times harder to track. There are no persistence cookies. We need to acknowledge the problem and develop a plan of attack to provide consumers with more *relevant* advertising messaging."

If you can identify a mobile consumer by time spent, data plan, content consumed, handset type, and so on, this allows you to generate a behavioral match. This profile can be expanded and honed in two ways:

1. Extrapolate through overlaying matching grouping in third-party data.
2. By accurately using one-to-one match keys such as a unique phone number or e-mail address.

"The goal," says Bell, "is to get a holistic picture of the consumer. Take the blindfold off and provide a better mobile experience for this consumer and, in doing, more value to the advertiser. It took six to seven years to evolve this on the web. The industry needs to work hard to make mobile as effective."

There is a magic line here. Does contextual advertising breach (what Spanish law refers to as) the "right to be forgotten"? When inaccurate information about an individual appears on the web, should the owner have control of this information? While Google and others call this censorship and refuse to intervene, it does draw into question whether an anonymous advertising profile that does not invoke an individual's name and identity but does attribute associated advertising based on her history may be embarrassing and drive consumers to call for the right to be forgotten.

Unquestionably, mobile is all about relevant messaging. This book has fifty-six references to *targeting,* but only forty-nine references to *impulse* (presumably the core thesis). In Jacob Wirth, the 140-year-old Boston drinking hole where I wrote a chunk of this chapter and had one of the nicer stouts in memory, there is a wood

carving at the back of the mahogany bar with a monogram reading "suum cuique" (to each his own). It seemed a very apt message. Mobile gives us new tools to personally target information, data, and advertising to the consumer in a contextual, just-in-time fashion. Marco Argenti, global head of media at Nokia, calls this context "the new URL."

"It is the most valuable insight we have into the mobile consumer," he insists. "Where are they? What are their interests? Nail this, and you had a one-to-one personal channel." The content owner needs to reach the consumer in context: to each her own.

If you can target, the phone is an exceptionally effective advertising destination. Unlike PCs, no one shares a mobile phone, everyone has his own, says Joy Liuzzo from InsightExpress. "As the device and platform evolved, mobile advertising became more refined and presented a unique medium for advertisers for three reasons: lack of clutter on the device; ads are proportionally larger on the screen; and engagement with the device, or the 'nose-to-screen' factor.

"Taking these factors into account," she continues, "we conducted a study comparing online and mobile advertising effectiveness. InsightExpress found mobile campaign norms were four and a half to five times higher than online norms against measures of unaided awareness, aided awareness, ad awareness, message association, brand favorability, and purchase intent."

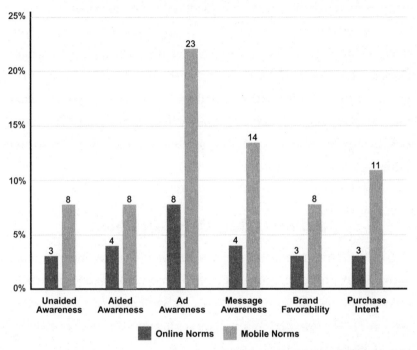

**Campaign Effectiveness Brand Metric Deltas:
Mobile Versus Online (November 2007–December 2010)**

Source: InsightExpress's Mobile Consumer Research, Dec. 2010

Startling is the 12 percent purchase intent for mobile campaigns compared to a paltry 2 percent for online campaigns. (Of course, we acknowledge that this 12 percent is a fraction of a second mobile engagement, whereas the 2 percent corresponds to a more thoughtful decision-making period online that can last hours, if not days.)

The mobile ad networks continue to sell mobile as a siloed buy, mainly because brand agencies continue to buy mobile as a siloed buy. As one mobile network executive told me, its sales team camps out in the lobby of buying agencies, handing out cupcakes

and hoping to take a senior team leader out for drinks to close a buy. There is no time, thought, or inclination to consider what happens after the impression is loaded on the network.

This is a disservice to mobile media that has the ability to drive value beyond the consumer eyeball to the shopper's wallet. Google's interest in the Mobile Wallet is the ability to provide targeted offers and information based on the user's commerce behavior. That content will drive high advertising value. Google knows that being close to payment and purchase intent will interest digital media buyers.

Advertising Driving Sales

Can online advertisement accelerate mobile advertisement? I asked Jason Spero, head of business development from AdMob/Google. (We were at the Shop.org conference in San Francisco, where every second retail presentation involved some mobile widget or insight.)

"The parallels are there, but time shifted," he said. "We're now transacting on mobile, but in a less sophisticated way to the online of the 2000s. We're living in dog years. One mobile year is seven or more online years."

We will soon catch up and probably exceed online, but will the mobile version look substantially different? Spero explained that there are basic aspects of mobile commerce that will benefit from online standards. We now know that online tracking and cookies are essential requirements. We must know where we want mobile commerce to be. This will accelerate the process. But there has to be a natural period of learning and experimentation.

Will the two ever reach parity? Is online advertising and commerce just at level C and mobile at level A, or do the fundamentals

that we see with the impulse behavior make it a different channel?

When AdMob launched an early program for 1-800-Flowers .com, it was initially seen as a success and then a failure. Spero explained that within twenty-four hours, the client loved mobile, then hated mobile. "Our mobile click-to-call campaign flooded their call center. This was good. But the leads were 'unqualified crap.' This was bad.

"The insight was that mobile obviously worked but differently to online. We need to refine the channel. AdMob is now using this learning. We now vet the user, then drive to click-to-call. Conversion is still high and more targeted, equaling more commerce."

During that period, 1-800-Flowers.com was selling no more than a few thousand dollars via the mobile channel. Into the 2010s, however, this number is well north of $1 million and growing significantly.

Understanding digital is a good first step to developing a mobile strategy, but more important, we need to understand what natively works and what does not work in mobile. AdMob refined and improved its acquisition model to drive more effective conversion. How do brands or retailers use mobile advertising to target, qualify, get reach, frequency, and drive sales?

It is exciting that mobile ads outperform online ads on recall (the ability of the consumer to remember the advertisement); however, mobile can be about more than simply branding. When a media planner buys mobile impressions on an ad network or from a publisher, is she simply diversifying the brand's reach into a new channel, or is the media planner implicitly asking for something new? Are we as a mobile industry underdelivering?

"I am buying mobile, which is a few feet from the mall and the cash register. What can mobile do given this proximity?"

There is a hopeful industry whisper that the move from analog dollars to digital dimes may possibly bounce back to "mobile dollars." If mobile can offer a qualitative leap in value that online so quickly and mercilessly cannibalized, we all may be making money again.

It is no secret that online dimes are not enough anymore. I was at the one of the Interactive Advertising Bureau's keynote addresses in Carlsbad, California, where the audience gasped as the entire sixty minutes was devoted to why pennies on advertising impressions could no longer support premium publishers, and a *WSJ*-type pay wall was the only salvation for the industry.

But maybe the industry needs to consider other measurement metrics beyond the impression. There is no question that push-media metrics such as CPM are valuable measurement tools, but mobile measurement can accurately tackle "place" of engagement, "quality" of engagement, "duration" of engagement, and the holy grail of "conversion" to high ROI destinations. Additionally, mobile, if it is bought correctly, can add these metrics to other siloed media verticals.

Apple to Apples: Mobile Ad Standards

But to start, we have to measure a mobile impression, and to do this we have to answer basic questions. What is a mobile impression? Is this measured client side or server side? Do we account for the constraints on the existing mobile browser or push for online measurement standards?

Whatever the industry decides, we unquestionably need uniform measurement standards. It is essential that the mobile CPM is given the credibility of its mature cousin the online CPM. The

Interactive Advertising Bureau (IAB) and the Mobile Marketing Association (MMA), with the help of the Media Rating Council (MRC), made this happen. The key trade groups were huddled for months on a joint task force, holding regular conference calls working out a model to extend online measurement codes to mobile. The result is a mobile measurement standard—the ultimate result may be a conflated digital measurement standard.

When this measurement standard hit the street in Barcelona in 2011, buyers breathed a collective sigh of relief that a click is a click is a click, and display and messaging impressions would have an auditable guideline. The online large-screen digital budget would be extended to mobile, and money would flow more freely into this emerging buy.

Unquestionably, this is what the market needs: mobile metrics will become part of the planning process. Brands will not simply launch a mobile campaign and figure out how to measure it later. They will plan metrics based on campaign goals (hopefully). This is exactly what new-generation mobile ad networks require, and in due course, dollars will flow and CPM rates will rise.

Then what? Traditional media planners have started to acknowledge that their push media is not as effective as billed because it is either not hitting the consumer or does not have the authenticity of social media to reinforce positive recall. We need to seek benchmarks or norms that are appropriate and relevant to the industry and/or specific type of campaign; relevant to the mobile consumer's behavior; and relevant to the medium. As Chetan Sharma, an industry pundit, accurately advocates, mobile can provide measurement to a wide array of consumer behavior that is way beyond the impression. I paraphrase:

1. Mobile delivers the right message to the right consumer.
2. Mobile delivers contextual, targeted messaging (location, carrier profile, self-selection).
3. Mobile measures the quality and duration of engagement.
4. And most important, mobile connects the dots, helping with customer conversion to last-mile ROI destinations such as PoS.

Sharma says, "Ad networks that are positioned to provide measurements and solution offerings on the above metrics will be able to rise above the noise and offer more compelling value propositions over the long term."

The m-shopper is media savvy. She understands (implicitly) that brands and retailers require a value exchange. To engage and drive a path to purchase, the advertiser needs to be relevant and have an authentic, honest voice. With these ingredients, purchase intent across all categories will outperform online advertising norms:*

Those are good numbers in any ledger.

* InsightExpress, "Campaign Effectiveness Brand Metrics Vertical: Mobile X Times More Effective Than Online" (November 2007–December 2009).

8 MOBILE RULES TO BUILD BY . . .

Thank you for bearing with me this far. In the spirit of the impulse economy and impulse consumption, here is an elementary checklist you may want to reference as you build out and manage your commerce strategy:

❑ **Leverage Existing Consumer Behavior**

How many conference panels have I attended where "This is the year of mobile" is followed by: "We just need to educate the consumer"? It is pure hubris to say that you will "educate" the user, who is far more advanced intuitively than a pack of marauding mobile experts.

Shoppers are using their phone for mobile web and SMS seamlessly throughout their day in our stores, hotels, and events. Our humble goal is to just try to "keep up" and capture a small piece of their conversation. They are way ahead of any marketing department.

❑ **Leverage the Largest Mobile Install Base**

Beware of snake-oil salesmen. Avoid anything that looks like a "shiny object" or "newfangled solution."

If consumers are using SMS and the mobile WEB as their main channels, then use them. When you think you should "walk" before you run, start at a crawl.

- Build your opt-in community.
- Buy some mobile advertising inventory.
- Use both to drive conversion solutions.

Reach and *frequency* are the two words that you need to continually use in the same sentence as *mobile advertising* and *marketing*.

In a world where Eric Schmidt says the consumer has two states—asleep and connected—the retailer and brand need to tie themselves to the consumer at all times. Start with simple list building and mobile CRM.

❑ **Leverage Existing Promotions and CRM Strategies**

IT will tell you this, but I will remind you: mobile should be an extension of business as usual in the store, street, or office. Do not start reinventing the world. Curb your enthusiasm.

Use mobile APIs (application programming interfaces) and tie them into your *existing* communication services and databases. E-mail, IVR (interactive voice response), SMS, and mobile web should all be fluid two-way opt-in channels.

❑ **What's Good for the Goose Needs to Be Good for the Gander**

Empower your "blue shirts" with the same mobile tools that the customer uses. Do not let the shopper have a more powerful tool to navigate your products than the salesclerk.

Remember Barclays COO Shaygan Kheradpir's expression the "commercialization of IT." Whether this means giving the Mercedes-Benz shopper a tablet when he enters the dealership or giving your clerk a smarter phone, the two worlds need to be on parity.

❑ **Count Clicks to Commerce**

Keep it simple. Very simple. Seems like an also-ran statement, but somewhere between concept and launch, many mobile-solution providers get struck by lightning and lose their simplicity gene.

The mobile consumer is on the run: you need one click-to-engage, one click-to-commerce, one click-to-bricks-and-mortar.

Add one step, and you have lost your shopper.

❑ **À La Carte Versus Quick Pick, Refill, Bundle . . .**

Counting clicks-to-commerce, à la carte, or deep menu shopping may not lead to optimal checkout. However, quick picks, saving favorites, or creating bundle value packs may help one-click conversion. Likewise, offering the monthly consumer refills and top-ups on cyclical products will drive more tonnage into the mobile basket.

❑ **Mobile Commerce Makes for Strange Bedfellows**

Given that mobile cuts across many verticals, note that mobile commerce connects partners that may never have been able to work together in the traditional world. American Express works with Facebook to deliver offers. Coke works with the wireless carrier to develop instant rebates. Handset manufacturers work with banks to enable phone-based wallets.

❑ **Suspend Belief**

In 2001 the wireless carrier did not believe that subscribers would pay for simple daily content such as jokes and horoscopes. Well, the service was a huge success. Lesson: suspend common sense with mobile services—the mobile consumer will opt in on impulse and pay for convenience.

❑ **Make It an Intimate, Personal, One-to-One Channel**

Though it may seem obvious, if you forget and build your service incorrectly, you will dramatically lose your hard-earned shopper opt-in. While permission-based marketing SMS has a nearly 100 percent view-rate (buzz-to-view time will amaze the most jaded CMO), SMS also has an equally high opt-out rate (if the viewed message is not what the subscriber expected).

The channel is digital gold. The shopper is now including you alongside her personal messages. You need to make a commitment to be as targeted and contextual as possible.

❑ **Make It a "Trojan" Channel**

For brands, allow your consumer to reach you directly for product and service information. In a world where you know

more about your brand than the in-store salesperson, allow consumers to search, surf, or text that product directly and learn why they need to buy it *now*.

Just as brands allow customers to text their products and engage at the moment of interest, every product can be the in-aisle expert guiding the potential consumer reviews, insights, and tips.

Additionally, allow the shopper to use this channel to post reviews, insights, and tips to you. Use it for pop surveys to gauge just-in-time feedback.

❑ Go So Lo

Be leery of social media third-party applications that try to drive acquisition and drive-to-aisle. The goal is not only to incentivize "check-in" at a store, restaurant, club, or hotel, but for the brand or retail to own a direct, long-term relationship with the shopper. Do not be disintermediated.

❑ Make It Horizontal

Mobile is a perfect medium to add to your existing media touch points. In a world where most of the media plan is bought as vertical push media, mobile is often pull. It allows the consumer to text, scan, and tap for information, rewards, and incentives off all your media touch points.

❑ Tell the Shopper

Mobile does not exist without a clear call to action. In Andy Warhol's twentieth-century words, "I never read. I just look at pictures." So do shoppers. Use strong iconography and segregated starbursts to signal them to use their phones.

❑ Security?

Encryption and payment standards make wireless an unwieldy commerce tool. With private data such as location, profile, and banking information floating through the cloud and over near field communication tags, there is sure to be multiple security abuses. Proceed with caution and in the company of seasoned industry experts.

❑ CMO = Chief Mobile Officer

We have established that consumer engagement and "impulse" conversion are the hallmarks of mobile. But to evangelize this across the organization may need more than one department or marketing manager pushing "horizontal integration" initiatives.

If the organization is committed to mobile, it may want to consider establishing a new position that works across the organization to drive mobile efforts. MTV, Microsoft, and the Weather Channel have roles that work to make mobile an integrated success across all screens and across all departments.

Building a homogeneous vision for mobile across the organization takes time. Remember: "9 women x one month do not make a baby."

❑ Innovation

Remember that your brand is not necessarily a mobile brand. Your job is not to become known as a mobile innovator. Remember Gartner's Hype Cycle. When it comes to the question of your mobile strategy, I would recommend responding with the following sage advice:

"Next year run the solutions you probably should
have run *last* year."

❑ Invest Flexibly

Mobile may be a moving target, but it is an unmistakable
target. Bob Parker from IDC Retail Insights says that his clients
have moved from "Should we invest in mobile?" to "What do
we spend money on in mobile?" "They end up sinking their
spend into option-based investment. They are basically hedg-
ing their mobile bets."

To paraphrase Georg Wilhelm Friedrich Hegel (a pre-
mobile German philosopher), who said that history makes the
man, not the inverse, well, *mobile consumers make the solution,
we do not*. Keep your ear to the ground and invest flexibly.

❑ Use Numbers. Talk ROI

Retailers live and die by results and numbers. For mobile to suc-
ceed, the industry must bring concrete return-on-investment
calculators to meetings. The industry must show the client
the number of mobile opt-ins year one, two, three. Walk the
would-be mobile client through:

1. Average mobile transaction rate
2. Average spend per shopper for mobile
3. Average margin percent
4. Total sales
5. Cost of mobile campaign
6. Total profit from mobile

❑ **Test It**

No one expects the retailer or brand to attach ClipCams to the glasses of prospective mobile shoppers to record and analyze their behavior, but the industry does mandate focus groups that try to understand shopper general MO. Finger-to-the-wind mobile strategies will fail.

Steve Jobs, Apple's former CEO, was quoted in *Fast Company* magazine as having said (obviously likening himself to Henry Ford), "If I'd have asked people what they wanted, they would've said a faster horse." Apple's game-changing products did not come out of focus groups or quantitative research; they came from insights into human behavior.

Yes, one shopper has little insight into her behavior, but the brand or service must run focus groups with shoppers to try to gain insight into their group behavior.

Finally, understand that mobile is a necessary evil. It is a needed shopping tool that in many ways distracts from the optimal shopping experience. The ideal mobile shopping utility would not inhibit mobility. Future mobile device technology and form factor may allow for the shopper to stand upright again.

There are many more things to add to this list but if you have got this far, you can begin to add your own insights as you explore mobile and join the members-only A-list of "mobile experts" that have the hubris of authoring their own list—and book.

Initialism and Acronym Hell

Advertising Lingo

CPA Cost per thousand acquisitions.

CPC Cost per thousand clicks.

CPM Cost per thousand impressions.

CRM Customer relationship management.

DOOH Digital-out-of-home media.

Off-line interactive Interactive media indirectly tethered to the Internet.

Online interactive Interactive media tethered to the Internet.

OOH Out-of-home media (billboards, bus shelters, etc.).

Pull media Media measured based on interactive impression.

Push media Media measured based on passive impression.

ROA Return on advertising.

ROI Return on investment.

Retail Lingo

Clearinghouses A third-party organization that settles coupons or prepaid fees.

CPG Consumer-packaged goods (Coke, P&G).

Detailer A person who checks brand display media on behalf of the advertiser.

End cap In-store advertising at the end of the aisle or adjacent to the shelf.

EPP Electronic proof of purchase (loyalty card, 2-D code scan, etc.).

FMOT First moment of truth (moment of selecting a product in a store).

PIN Personal or unique identification number.

POP Point of purchase (media in the store environment).

PoS Point of sale (payment terminal and cash register).

Shelf talkers In-store and in-aisle advertising.

Shopper marketing The marketing science of engaging the shopper in the store.

Spiff Rewarding a salesperson for learning or using a product.

ZMOT Zero moment of truth (moment of loyalty to a product on the web).

Mobile and Tech Lingo

API Application programming interface.

Bluecasting Provide digital media to suitable media-provisioning-enabled devices over Bluetooth.

Bluetooth Proprietary open wireless standard for short-distance exchange of machine-to-machine data.

GPS Global Positioning System.

LBS Location-based services.

Lo-so Location and social integration.

LTE Long-term evolution wireless network.

MIDI standard musical instrument digital interface.

MMS Multimedia messaging services.

Monotone Monophonic tonality ringtones.

MVNO Mobile Virtual Network Operator (Boost, Virgin).

NFC Near field communication contactless protocol.

OEM Original equipment manufacturer (specifically referring to handset manufacturers).

Off deck Digital content that is open and discovered by the consumer.

On deck Digital content that is controlled and curated.

OneAPI A set of carrier APIs consolidated to accelerate application development.

OTA Over-the-air delivery of mobile content.

Polyphonic tone Polyphonic tonality ringtones.

RFID An electronic tag that uses radio waves to transfer data.

SDK Software development kit.

Smartpipe Enablers Identified business models that require APIs services.

SMS Short messaging services.

True tones/master tones Full digitalized audio ringtones.

WAP Wireless Application Protocol.

Organizations

GREC Global Retail Executive Council.

GS1 Global trade body for bar code and 2-D code standards.

GSMA Global trade body representing the interests of mobile operators worldwide.

IAB Interactive Advertising Bureau.

MARI Marketing at Retail Initiative.

MEF Mobile Entertainment Forum.

MMA Mobile Marketing Association.

MRC Media Rating Council.

POPAI In-store marketing association.

WAC Wholesale Applications Community.